Praise for *The Insanity Hoax*

"In this original and passionate work, Judith Schlesinger takes on one of the great Western myths—the mad, tortured genius—and serves up her painstaking research on the subject with equal portions of wit, wisdom, and criticism. The myth, she shows, is encrusted in our ways of viewing creativity, fed to us by an unthinking media, and fueled by the self-serving 'analyses' of so-called experts. Her book is chock-full of facts that set the record straight and insights that challenge us to think for ourselves. This is an emancipatory book—and a good read."

—**David Cohen**, PhD, Professor of Social Work and Distinguished Tocqueville-Fulbright Chair, Florida International University

"Do you have to be crazy to be creative? Nowadays, most people seem to think so, but the evidence points in the other direction. How, then, did this mistaken notion worm its way into our collective consciousness, and how much damage has it done to our understanding of art and artists? In *The Insanity Hoax*, Judith Schlesinger exposes the exaggerations and falsehoods of the ever-seductive myth of the mad genius—and explains why so many people prefer it to the truth. Anyone who believes that madness is the flip side of the coin of creativity needs to read this book."

—**Terry Teachout**, drama critic for the *Wall Street Journal* and author of *Pops: A Life of Louis Armstrong*

"Judith Schlesinger has hit the bull's-eye with *The Insanity Hoax*. She passionately and completely debunks the biased, pervasive notion that artists are 'crazier' than the rest of humankind, showing us in highly engaging prose how they stare human frailties squarely in the face for the benefit of all. Thank you, Judith."

—**Shelton G. Berg**, Dean and Patricia L. Frost Professor of Music, Frost School of Music, University of Miami

"A rare combination of trenchant observations, penetrating insight, vivid writing, and great humor, Judith Schlesinger rips to shreds the 'common wisdom' that creative people and people of genius are more likely than others to be 'mentally ill' (however one defines that term) or even that their mental illness is responsible for their brilliance. A must-read for everyone who cares or thinks about a life of creativity, about emotional pain, or both."

—**Paula J. Caplan**, PhD, clinical and research psychologist and author of *They Say You're Crazy: How the World's Most Powerful Psychiatrists Decide Who's Normal*

"*Hoax* is fascinating, insightful, and surprisingly funny. Judith is a gifted writer whose observations are infused with a deep knowledge of music, history, and psychology. She is a creative and witty thinker—imagine a far more intellectual Erma Bombeck exploding the myths of psychiatry and culture."

—**Chris Brubeck**, "fairly sane and highly functional" jazz musician and classical composer

"At last, there is someone to tackle the Mad Genius legend. Judith Schlesinger's *The Insanity Hoax* picks up the mantle for unfairly stereo-typed artists—and does so with passion, wit, and incisive critique. Highly recommended."

—**James C. Kaufman**, PhD, Professor of Psychology, California State University at San Bernadino, and President-Elect of the American Psychological Association Division for Aesthetics, Creativity and the Arts

"Judith Schlesinger lets all the hot air out of the over-inflated psychobab-ble-for-profit balloon, wielding a deft, sometimes deadly scalpel fueled by acute insight, humor, and a delightfully readable prose style. As a bonus for this reader, she does justice to jazz and its makers."

—**Dan Morgenstern**, Director, Institute of Jazz Studies, author of *Living with Jazz*, and winner of eight Grammy Awards

"In her skillful and entertaining dissection of the mad genius myth, she deconstructs the pseudoscience used to support it, while illuminating the deep cultural functions that this myth can serve for the society, the geniuses themselves, and for the rest of us less creative and more normally mad. Schlesinger tells a story worth reading."

—**Stuart A. Kirk**, DSW, Professor of Social Welfare, UCLA Luskin School of Public Affairs, and coauthor of *The Selling of DSM*, *Making Us Crazy*, and the forthcoming *Mad Science*

"With persuasive reasoning, wit, and extensive documentation, Judith Schlesinger dispels the myth of the 'mad genius.'"

—**Bill Kirchner**, jazz musician, historian, producer, educator, and editor of *The Oxford Companion to Jazz*

"Judith Schlesinger's new book, *The Insanity Hoax*, is a fun read as well as a valuable and well-documented scholarly discourse. The mythology of the artist as a mentally impaired nutcase (and by that definition a worthless member of society) has always been an appealing stereotype to keep artists' place in society (and their salaries) at the bottom of the curve. Dr. Schlesinger's book explains, with clarity and brilliance, why this uninformed way of thinking about creative people is no longer valid. It's a refreshing relief to know that artists whose work is of enduring value are no longer doomed to being equated with the stoned-out losers who appear on reality TV."

—**David Amram**, composer, conductor, multi-instrumentalist, and author of *Vibrations: A Memoir*

"Judith Schlesinger makes her case with wry wit, wisdom, and passion that the symptoms of madness and just plain old creativity have long been joined in an inappropriate dance. There are many jazz musicians referred to in the book that have skirted both of these labels. She provides true insight into their inner creative lives."

—**Fred Hersch**, award-winning jazz pianist and composer

"This work is a corrective to unwarranted folk beliefs and misleading and erroneous research regarding a connection between creativity and mental illness."

—**Albert Rothenberg**, MD, Professor of Psychiatry, Harvard Medical School, and author of *Creativity and Madness: New Findings and Old Stereotypes*

"Decades of scientific study have shown that there is no connection between creativity and mental illness. In fact, there is substantial evidence that creative people are more healthy than average. Schlesinger's book does an excellent job of summarizing the history of the mad genius myth, and of debunking the few published studies that are often cited as evidence for a link. If you are tempted to believe in a link between insanity and creativity, you absolutely must read this book first."

—**Keith Sawyer**, PhD, Professor of Psychology and Education, Washington University in St. Louis, and author of *Group Genius: The Creative Power of Collaboration* and *Explaining Creativity*

"Judith Schlesinger's wonderful new book does a superb job of debunking popular myths about 'crazy artists' and redressing the mental health industry's practice of pathologizing creative people. This book should be required reading for creative and performing artists, their teachers, their therapists, and anyone who loves them. Not to be missed!"

—**Eric Maisel**, PhD, creativity coach and author of *Rethinking Depression* and *The Van Gogh Blues*

the INSANITY HOAX

Exposing the Myth
of the Mad Genius

JUDITH SCHLESINGER, PhD

Ardsley-on-Hudson, New York

Published by Shrinktunes Media
PO Box 260
Ardsley-on-Hudson, NY 10503
www.theinsanityhoax.com

Cover photograph by Michael Rosen
Cover and book design by Sandra Jonas

Printed in the United States of America

17 16 15 14 13 12   2 3 4 5 6 7

Publisher's Cataloging-in-Publication Data

Schlesinger, Judith.
    The insanity hoax : exposing the myth of the mad genius / Judith Schlesinger.
  Ardsley-on-Hudson, NY : Shrinktunes Media, 2012.

    p. cm.

    ISBN: 9780983698241

    Includes bibliographical references and index.

    1. Genius and mental illness.

BF423 .S35 2012   153.98 —dc23

2011910967

For Carla,
Friede at last

Contents

Applause

This book has been in progress for so long that some early supporters left this life before it was published. I like to think they are enjoying its emergence at last, even from their considerable distance. This list begins with my dear parents, Joe and Bertha, and includes Gene Lees, Steve Allen, Eddie (Haydie) Higgins, Les Line, and Jim Eaves.

Much gratitude to my fiancé, Norm Lotz, for his loving patience during many months of obsessive behavior. Kudos to other sustainers Steve (Heevus) Barlas, Thom Filo, Brian Gair, Lynn Eustance, Priscilla Hindley, Donna Kaufman, Richard Miller, Michael Rosen, Barbara Sfraga, and Ellen Theg.

Many thanks to my reader friends for their invaluable suggestions and support: Dr. Ron Carducci, Billy Goda, Fred Hersch, Dr. Dee Jacob, and Dorothy Moore. Hats off to Dr. James Kaufman for his inspiration and generosity, and to "book midwife" Sandra Jonas for her excellent coaching and design and fierce pursuit of error.

Finally, I salute the dedicated musicians I've been privileged to know who prove that it's possible to be exceptionally creative and eminently sane at the same time. Among them are Shelly Berg, Gene Bertoncini, Chris Brubeck, John Clayton, Meredith d'Ambrosio, Taylor Eigsti, Peter Eldridge, Lorraine Feather, Paulinho Garcia, Jeff Hamilton, Fred Hersch (again), Jay Leonhart, Bill Mays, Kate McGarry, Mike Metheny, Kim Nazarian, Lynn Seaton, and Sean Smith.

Prelude

There are just as many disturbed and self-destructive bakers, but critics do not analyze their cakes.

                ~ Anatole Broyard

THOSE CRAZY MUSICIANS. THEY STAY up all night, sleep all day, and forget to pay the rent even when they have it. Moody and unpredictable, promiscuous and irresponsible, they live to play—which isn't really work. Whether a horn player pickled in alcohol or a chick singer addicted to drugs and abusive men, they aren't like the rest of us. Driven to serve a different god, they're willing to forsake everything for a few shining moments on the stage—though they never had much stability to surrender, which is why they chose that crazy life in the first place. We may envy their gift, but never its price. This is the story of the mad genius, a myth born in antiquity and likely to be with us forever.

Even as a kid, I noticed the general expectation that creative lives would be stormier and ultimately more tragic than those of ordinary mortals. When I studied classical piano, I experienced the melancholy, inconsolable Chopin and the thunderous passion of the lonely Beethoven. I was a rock fan when Jimi Hendrix, Janis Joplin, and Jim Morrison were all murdered by their inner demons. I remember people

1

saying this was inevitable, since it's always the brightest stars who flare up and burn out, right?

Later, when I found my way to jazz, I encountered yet another tribe of brilliant and doomed ones, trapped in their own thicket of stereotypes about the antisocial and dissipated musician. By then I had gotten used to the two words "mad genius" spoken without a breath—or a thought—between them.

The roll of legendary troubled musicians is a long and familiar one, from Beethoven and Berlioz to Charlie Parker and Billie Holiday. Part of the draw of a Judy Garland concert was the high-wire suspense of whether she'd get through it; her daughter Liza Minnelli inspired the same mix of loyalty and voyeurism. Certainly, the thrill of watching talented people fail is responsible for a big chunk of *American Idol*'s prodigious success.

While the "humilitainment" of reality shows is relatively new, creative instability has always attracted a crowd. Since musicians can let go in a way others cannot, they often provide a vicarious display of raw feeling. And when your product is your soul, personal disaster is more likely, so highly creative people are always at special risk.

Or are they?

Plato seemed to think so, equating inspiration with "divine madness," or what the Muses bring when they inhabit the artist. "All the good poets are not in their right mind when they make their beautiful songs," he said. Although Plato's madness was benign and not clinical, he did introduce the idea of artists as helpless puppets, animated by mystical forces they can neither summon nor stop. And when Aristotle claimed that "all great men are melancholic," he completed the portrait that endures to this day: the miserable gifted person who's only marginally in control of himself.

Although both Plato and Aristotle meant something else altogether, as we will see in the pages ahead, the doomed artist is a popular historical figure and likely to remain so. Four centuries ago, Shakespeare had a virtual franchise of tragic heroes who were enjoying greatness until some inherent flaw detonated and brought them down. Today, that same fiery arc is traced in book, TV, and movie biographies of exceptional talents. Even Netflix, in organizing its customers' viewing preferences, offers "tortured genius" as a category of story line—right next to "talking animals."

Madness and the Media

IT'S DISMAYING HOW eager we are to find something wrong with creative lives. The *New York Times* reliably cranks out headlines like "How Inner Torment Feeds the Creative Spirit" and "The Latest of the Jazz Weirdos," which includes this revelation: "It's not that rock and classical music haven't had their own share of weirdos, but jazz's relationship to weirdness is particularly pronounced" (1). Reviewing a play about Judy Garland, their theater critic casually refers to "that perilous, bipolar energy that so often animates great performers" (2). In 2003, I signed up for their "news tracker" service to notify me whenever the mad genius topic appeared in their pages. These alerts arrive every few days, reminding me that the mad genius idea is alive and well, and thoroughly embedded in society.

Other publications agree: in 1998, the prestigious *Utne Reader* ran the story "The Genius and the Nut: Embracing Disordered Brilliance." That same year, *Esquire* published an interview with brilliant trumpeter Tom Harrell, one of the few jazz musicians with an obvious disorder (his diagnosis is schizophrenia), informing us that "in the world of jazz . . . abnormal behavior has always been the tradition." The *U.S. News & World Report* asked, "Was Emily Dickinson a Genius or Just Bonkers?" and *Rolling Stone* casually confirmed "the thin line between psychotics and geniuses [who] all tread the same razor's edge" (3).

Across the pond, the BBC announced that "creative minds mimic schizophrenia" and that "creativity is known to be associated with an increased risk of depression, schizophrenia, and bipolar disorder." Back home, William Cromie of the *Harvard University Gazette* stated that creativity and mental illness "seem to be linked, particularly in artists, musicians, and writers," while psychologists were advised by their in-house monthly that "schizophrenia may be the origin of jazz" (4). And leave it to *The Simpsons* to spoof this whole thing, as when Bart asks, "Who knew that a troubled person could be creative?" (5).

Not only is this indoctrination broad, but it starts early. Magic Tree House is a popular children's series that introduces Leonardo da Vinci in Book #38, *Monday with a Mad Genius* (6). At no point does this little book or its companion "nonfiction research guide" explain what "mad" means or why Da Vinci was labeled that way. The focus is only on his many creative ideas, which encourages young people (as well as their parents) to believe that "mad genius" is a natural descriptor for anyone especially brilliant or inventive. And since this series appears in several languages, it ensures that this message spreads around the world.

Even *JazzTimes*—allegedly the musician's friend—perpetuated a particularly scary exaggeration of the mad creative idea. In "Music, Mental Illness, and Prison," their wildly inaccurate cover article of October 2002, we learn that jazz musicians are especially prone to that "treacherous bipolar disease," which—if it doesn't kill them or send them to jail—will require "daily therapy and long-term assisted living." This was destructive as well as ridiculous, but the editors refused to set the record straight despite the urging of several jazz experts (7).

To be fair, the media must feed the public its favorite snacks in order to survive; as jazz author Richard Sudhalter describes it,

> The public loves the romance, the outlaw charm, of being a musician . . . but woe betide the writer who . . . treats him as anything other than a walking pathology or some kind of raffish exotic. (8)

Moreover, some jazz aficionados actually view self-destruction as a prerequisite for genius:

> If a piano player could drink a pint of scotch during a recording

session, or had a heroin habit, or an abusive streak, for American jazz fans such behavior has as much to do with his greatness as does his grasp of harmony or rhythm. (9)

These expectations make the healthy musician boring in comparison. Reed player Bud Shank tells of losing valuable free publicity because he was insufficiently deranged:

I had two different jazz authors spend a lot of time and a lot of research doing a book about me. Both of them got halfway through it and quit because they couldn't find anything wrong with me. I haven't been in jail, I haven't been an alcoholic, I haven't done anything nasty—so in their eyes, as far as what sells books about jazz musicians, there was nothing to write about. Ever since Van Gogh cut his ear off, everybody thinks an artist has to be a hurt artist. It's like you're no good otherwise. (10)

Writer Gene Lees, who knew Dizzy Gillespie well, explained how the well-known serenity and warmth of the great trumpeter compromised his reputation for greatness:

Dizzy loved to laugh, and to make others laugh. But jazz was in the phase of being discovered as a Serious Art Form, and the antics of Dizzy didn't seem to be helping the cause. Bird [Charlie Parker], dark, doomed and remote, made a better icon for idolaters. This, too, without question, contributed to the diminished perception of Gillespie's importance. (11)

Finally, even jazz musicians themselves may buy into the necessity of creative suffering and isolation. Saxophonist Johnny Griffin explained his fate in an interview: "I'm not really from this planet. I did something wrong on my planet, and they sent me here to pay my dues" (12).

Cinema Un-vérité

MOVIEMAKERS ALSO LOVE to link creativity and madness. In *Shine*, many facts about pianist David Helfgott's life are twisted to fit the stereotypes, distortions that are detailed in his sister Margaret's book, *Out of Tune: David Helfgott and the Myth of Shine* (1998), as well as in a psychiatric article subtitled "Never Spoil a Good Story with the Facts" (13). After a long and bitter struggle with the producers, the Helfgott family got a legal disclaimer inserted into the credits. However, since it appears after 279 others have scrolled by, most viewers will miss it—and thus have no reason to doubt anything they just saw. Meanwhile, the mad genius mystique supported an eighteen-city tour and brisk sales of David's CD, despite unanimous critical dismay at his playing.

David's wife, Gillian, continues to control his public statements, carefully protecting every fiction. This was obvious in two television documentaries I saw, in 1998 and 2011, when she kept interrupting to answer questions that were addressed to him. Gillian also owns the copyrights to all his letters, so they cannot be published by their recipients. "I believe he doesn't have much opportunity to express himself as he would really like to," Margaret told me in an email. Describing her rare meetings with David, she wrote, "At these precious moments, it's as if *Shine* never existed and never intruded into our lives to create such havoc" (14). Meanwhile, his handlers continue to position him somewhere between Forrest Gump and the Elephant Man.

In 2001, *A Beautiful Mind* took similar liberties with mathematician John Nash's life. Just as *Shine* deliberately omits Helfgott's first marriage (to Claire Papp) to dramatize his isolation, filmmakers tweak Nash's romantic history to bolster the "beauty and beast" theme of the doomed madman saved by the love of a good woman. They also downplay the fact that his best idea, for which he eventually won the Nobel Prize, came ten years *before* his breakdown and that he actually fared better once he resisted his diagnosis and discontinued medication (15).

But the spin was so appealing that it inspired the PBS special *A Brilliant Madness* (2002). The movie's title was later borrowed for a

2011 Baltimore Symphony concert called *Schumann's Beautiful Mind*. The "crazy composer concert" is a popular distortion that I find especially troubling; its manipulations are discussed in chapter 5.

The jazz cinema is also notoriously fond of the dissipated genius—as one writer puts it, "When jazz is allowed onto the screen, the pathologies are never far behind" (16). The clunky and dated *A Man Called Adam* (1966) contains every tragic cliché in the catalog, including defining Adam's appeal as "the sense of personal danger" he conveys to his audience. *Bird* (1988) portrays the sad life of bebop pioneer Charlie Parker, and *Round Midnight* (1986) presents a kamikaze composite of pianist Bud Powell and saxophonist Lester Young.

Then there's *The Prince of Cool*, a screenplay-in-waiting about the drug-addicted trumpeter Chet Baker, who finally and mysteriously vaulted out of a second-story window in Amsterdam. Despite interest from Leonardo de Caprio and Johnny Depp, this project is still treading water. As far as I know, no feature films are in the works about stable and prolific jazzers like Dizzy Gillespie, Dave Brubeck, Ray Brown, or Duke Ellington—nor are they likely to be.

Perhaps this is because pathology wins more prizes. On Broadway, Warren Leight's Tony-winning *Side Man* portrays jazz musicians as pathetic losers whose only reason to celebrate is somebody's first unemployment check (17). In *Proof*, the drama that won both the 2001 Pulitzer Prize and the Tony for Best Play, the math genius's daughter is terrified of inheriting his craziness along with his talent. This stereotypical tale became a 2005 film, attracting Gwynneth Paltrow and Anthony Hopkins for the major roles.

The Dawning of Doubt

BY NOW, EVERYONE knows that there's a "fine line between genius and madness"—if only because they hear it so often. But is there any *scientific* truth to it? Nope.

My first flickers of skepticism arrived in 1974 when I began graduate work in psychology and was shocked to find how much madness was rooted in guesswork. When the psychiatric reference bible—the *Diagnostic and Statistical Manual of Mental Disorders*, or DSM—publicly morphed from version III through the III-R to the IV (from 1980 to 1994), I had a front-row seat for the professional haggling that drives the definitions of mental "illness." But today, the American Psychiatric Association (APA) has closed the theater, since all participants working on the DSM-5, due in 2013, have had to sign a vow of secrecy.

The APA claims that participants merely signed a "Work Acceptance Form," not a confidentiality agreement—but download the form from their website, and you'll see that clause 6 is precisely that (18). So much for their "open and inclusive" process. Psychiatrist Robert Spitzer, who was the lead editor on the DSM-III, said the APA claimed it was protecting its property rights, as if anyone might dare to publish a pirated version of the copyrighted manual. "I think the real motivation was to keep control and minimize critiques," he said in a 2011 interview. "If people can't talk about it, they can't critique it" (19).

What isn't secret is how thoroughly the field itself is up for sale, given the zillions that pharmaceutical companies invest in professional organizations, self-help groups, seductive drug ads, and the bank accounts of especially useful psychiatrists. Big Pharm's power to dictate diagnosis mocks any claim that such decisions are based on science (for the most strenuous counterarguments, read virtually anything written by psychiatrist Thomas Szasz, who has produced dozens of books since his eye-opening first in 1961: *The Myth of Mental Illness*).

So—I thought—if psychiatric definitions were that susceptible to horse-trading and expectation, how could we be so sure that creative people were more disturbed than anyone else? Must all great art be wrestled out of personal misery, or are there more benign ways to explain its creation? One fine day the epiphany struck: the answer depends on who's asking the question.

This was evident in the arbitrary way those ancient rumors about creative madness had congealed into "fact." In the past thirty years, many psychologists, psychiatrists, and academics of all stripes have insisted on bundling genius with bipolar disorder—a chorus that legitimizes the public's suspicions and every media variation on this fascinating theme. But there's no compelling proof that creative people have more psychological problems than members of any other vocational group—and little interest in obtaining any.

For example, neither the National Institute of Mental Health (NIMH) nor the patient advocacy group Depression and Related Affected Disorders Association (DRADA, formerly the National Depressive and Manic-Depressive Association, or NDMDA) keeps tabs on the rate of mental illness by occupation. So when we hear that one in four U.S. adults suffers from mood disorders every year, we have no idea how many are dentists and how many are drummers. Moreover, there's no national data set on occupation and suicide, partly because only half of the states even include occupation on their death certificates (20).

In the past thirty years, a jumble of unrelated studies in the United States and worldwide have found high suicide rates in such wildly disparate groups as physicians, construction workers, sailors, miners, black crossing guards, and Swedish reindeer herders—or, they find no connection between suicide and occupation at all (21). But the cultural expectations about artists remain confident, making the heavy price of talent seem inevitable.

There's only one sure way to prove that creative people are more disturbed than the so-called non-creative (assuming that people utterly devoid of creativity actually exist): both creativity and madness must be clearly defined and measured, and the two groups compared in at least one rigorous, large-scale study. So far, this hasn't happened.

There was a chance, ten years ago, to pull one shining needle out of this haystack, but it was lost—probably forever, as explained in chapter 4. What remains is a mishmosh of weak studies that rely on ancient hearsay about the long deceased or on living participants who are either self-selected or handpicked, methods that compromise the outcome from the start. Moreover, their incompatible research designs make it impossible to fairly combine their results into convincing proof of anything. The very best they can be is suggestive.

At this point, the only absolute certainty in this enterprise is that some people create things that amaze those who cannot, whether it's because of godlike intervention, fortunate DNA, or subtle quirks in the wiring of the brain. But when you pile on all the popular mythology about the mad genius, you end up with a race of human hybrids who are simultaneously envied for their brilliance and pitied for their handicaps.

Where Does It Go?

ONE SUMMER, VERY early in my career, I had the opportunity to work one-on-one with a young inpatient in a psychiatric hospital. Although I was just a beginning graduate student, I was given complete freedom in meeting with E. three afternoons a week. I liked to think it was because of my obvious innate talents, but I suspect it had more to do with the fact that this twenty-six-year-old woman had already accumulated such a prodigious resume of diagnoses, treatments, and institutions that I probably couldn't do her much harm.

The suburban setting was graced with acres of beautiful woods and rolling lawns. E. and I would find some chairs in a quiet place and sit together, talking for hours. She told me about her family, her frustrations and dreams; I listened carefully and offered what I imagined were useful therapeutic responses. Despite her label of paranoid schizophrenia, we had perfectly lucid conversations, laced with humor—at least, until it was time for her midday meds.

A nurse with a tray would appear in the distance, looking around for E. And each time, the oddest thing happened: as the figure in white approached across the great lawn, E. would stop talking and begin folding into herself. Shoulders rounding, head hanging down, she even developed a twitch in her mouth and both hands. By the time the nurse arrived, E. had turned into the very picture of a heavily medicated inpatient—dazed, docile, and muttering incoherently. The nurse spoke to her as if she were a barely functioning toddler, handed her tiny paper cups of pills and water to empty, smiled, and walked away.

Once she was out of sight, our conversation resumed where we left off. Sometimes we'd walk over to the building with a decent Steinway piano, and E. would play Beethoven sonatas from memory. Beautifully. It was hard to believe that the fingers moving with such expert dexterity and eloquence were the same ones I'd just seen in helpless spasm.

I found this sequence of events completely baffling, and couldn't wait to ask my supervisor about it. He was a friendly staff psychiatrist who met with me an hour a week to offer guidance and support. But he had no explanation for E.'s transformation from coherent to crazy and back again, on cue. Nor would he answer when I asked, "If she has such a serious mental illness, where does it go?" A shrug was the best he could do.

I never did get a good answer to that question. And I still wonder what happened to that perceptive and talented young woman. Our conversations ended when she left the hospital for another, where she would undergo the newest treatment for schizophrenia: kidney dialysis. Back then, there was a theory that some element in the blood caused mental "illness," which could be "cured" by flushing it out—whatever it was. Given the procedure's drastic nature, participation was limited to those who'd tried everything else; their doctors also had to submit a video that "proved" they were sufficiently crazy to justify the risk. I'm sure E.'s performance was Oscar-worthy, but the treatment didn't work.

Decades later, dialysis has proven about as effective as the "bath of surprise" (another dead-end cure for mental "illness," described in chapter 4). But for me the questions remain: is this aberrant behavior caused by social expectations and training, or are we actually talking about some physical disease? If it is biological, where is it, and where does it go?

What Lies Ahead

LET ME SHOW my hand from the jump: I detest the patronizing caricature of the mad creative and how it devalues the artistic product. Despite the absence of clear proof that great talents are especially prone to bipolar disorder, they are supposed to live in dread of a ticking time bomb that could go off any minute. This is ironic, given the incessant commercial messages about medicating every personal difficulty ("Ask your doctor whether E-Z Cure is right for you!"), and the growth industry of celebrities who embrace the chic diagnosis du jour to boost a sagging profile or excuse their bad behavior. All this casual trafficking in psychopathology trivializes the suffering that genuine disorders can cause.

I believe that what distinguishes and drives the exceptionally gifted has less to do with any grand theory than with their own complex and private flowering. *The Insanity Hoax* is a call to honor that blossoming, rather than viewing it with suspicion. But please note: although this book is grounded in decades of careful scholarship, it's not a scientific tome—it's more of a slow-turning searchlight for illuminating the darker corners of the mad genius myth, with all their cobwebs and stardust.

I agree with the great philosopher Karl Popper, who said that identifying and dismantling myths is the first business of science. I also believe that science doesn't have to be stuffy.

In the chapters ahead, you'll see how linking creativity and madness is as futile as grabbing at clouds—and how that never seems to discourage anyone from trying. The searchlight then follows the mad genius from its ancient birth to its latest incarnation, examining the social currents that make it alternately desirable or dangerous, depending on the flow of the larger culture.

The Insanity Hoax also exposes the rickety pseudoscience the myth sits on, especially the popular work of its most influential advocates: psychiatrists Nancy Andreasen and Arnold Ludwig, and psychologist Kay Redfield Jamison. At the same time, it salutes the powerful incentives that will preserve the myth forever.

Let me be clear: I am not saying there are *no* creative people with genuine psychological problems, whether their diagnosis is bipolar disorder or anything else. Of course there are—just as there are erratic and unhappy lawyers and librarians, teachers and telemarketers. The distortion occurs when the great creatives are said to be *more* susceptible to this suffering than other groups, and studies are massaged to "prove" it.

I've always been intrigued by how this mad genius thing operates in the field of music—especially with jazz, which has been a cherished focus for most of my adult life. "Write what you know," they say, and this is where I live: as a fan, a friend, professional critic and columnist, therapist, performer, and, most recently, producer. So when real-life examples are called for, I draw them from the world I know best. At the same time, this book will be useful for creatives of any stripe—as well as for those who love them and want to understand them better—since so many of the dreams and challenges are the same.

One last note before the journey begins: people may define themselves as dedicated or "someday-when-I-have-time" creatives—and might even be unsung geniuses—while still making their living at unrelated but necessary day jobs. They may view creative freelancing as a luxury, which is ironic considering how little and inconsistently it usually pays. Other people make distinctions between those artists who provide "source"—composers, choreographers, and playwrights—and those who interpret this material: the singers, dancers, and actors. There are arguments to be made about differences in creativity and emotional vulnerability—or the lack thereof—but that's a smackdown for another day. Meanwhile, all these variations complicate the definition of a committed creative life, as well as the identification of genius. But nothing in this area is precise, as the following pages will prove.

I believe that creativity should be celebrated, not diagnosed. I hope this book will convince you as well—or at least make you think twice about it from now on.

PART ONE

Grabbing at Clouds

ONE

Creativity
Blind Men and Elephant Parts

Before I came here, I was confused about this subject. Having listened to your lecture, I am still confused—but on a higher level.

∼ Enrico Fermi

ACCORDING TO SOME ACCOUNTS, BEETHOVEN liked to pour water over his head and sing, becoming literally so immersed that he kept flooding his apartments and getting evicted. Did that reflect his madness, his genius, or his attempt to drown out the ominous buzz in his ears that began at age thirty? Jazz pianist Thelonious Monk would abruptly stop playing during performances and whirl like a dervish. Was his bizarre behavior proof of craziness or part of the showmanship he learned early on, while playing for a traveling tent show?

Creativity and madness are slippery things, hard to describe and impossible to quantify. Like pornography, we know them when we see them, but despite years of trying to wrestle them to the mat, there's still no universal definition or test for either one—and when they collide, they raise a whole new cloud of questions.

Which experts are correct: the ones who insist that "manic depression is almost indispensable to genius" (1), or those who claim that "we haven't found compelling evidence of a connection between mental illness and creativity" (2)? Like debates over the existence of God, this field offers more passion than proof; much of its certainty gleams with promise from a distance, but tends to vanish on approach.

For example, because nobody has pinpointed the wiring that enhances creativity, we can't know for certain whether it also increases the risk of pathology. These two variables are so enigmatic that each requires its own chapter (creativity first, madness next). Even then, this book will not explicate all their facets—just what happens when they are thrown together. And jazz, that wonderfully living and changing art form, will not be defined at all—there is too much ongoing fulmination about what it is, or isn't, which is beyond the scope of this enterprise.

Creative Components

MOST GOOD DICTIONARIES echo the grand *Oxford English*, which reveals that the word "creativity" didn't actually appear in print until 1875. Its relative recency is one small reason for all the confusion.

When creativity is confined to the ability to bring something new into being, it covers everything from concertos to childbirth. But go just one step further and the squabbling begins: team A argues that creativity stems from environmental factors, team B believes that the key is tucked deep inside the brain, while team C claims that they must interact in some mysterious way. It's that old blind-men-and-elephant thing where each person is firmly convinced that the pachyderm part he's holding is the entire truth.

The whole beast can be embraced at once with the "confluence" model, which acknowledges the convergence of numerous different elements (3). Psychologist Dean Simonton borrowed the term "stochastic process" from probability theory to characterize this interaction as mysterious (4). If it were only up to me, I'd stop right there and go out for coffee, but most readers might want a bit more than that. Be warned, however: if you go a'Googling for the definition of creativity, you'll get over nineteen million hits.

What follows are just two of the good ones:

1. Creativity is the ability to produce work that is both novel (original, unexpected) and appropriate (it works: it is useful or meets task constraints). (5)

2. Creativity is the interaction among aptitude, process, and environment by which an individual or group produces a perceptible product that is both novel and useful as defined within a social context. (6)

Unfortunately, such abstractions raise more questions than they answer. For instance, how do you define and measure these abilities, aptitudes, and processes? Does everyone agree on what they look like? And what does "useful" mean, anyway? Useful to whom? For what? And, who says?

"Novelty" is only part of the story, since creativity is far more than newness. So if we consider "quality" as well, who gets to judge that? Experts? Teachers? Peers? And by what criteria? Are there reliable assessments of artistic quality, and if so, can they ever calibrate the essence of beauty?

And while we're at it, who decides what's "appropriate" in a creative domain? Is "meeting task constraints" the best yardstick for that brilliant trumpet solo that just ignited the room? Shouldn't some intrinsic factors be considered as well? And if so, can we specify what they are, and how to identify them as they're flying by?

This is only some of the static on this channel, which also includes the paradox that successful creativity requires both nonconformity and social acceptance at the same time. Genius adds its own dynamic, because achievements at that level create "propulsive moments" that can smash through traditional boundaries to change a domain (7). But even that isn't reliable, since their progress may be blocked by the self-appointed guardians of a domain's "purity" who refuse to move it away from its past.

Here's another conundrum to consider: do people qualify as creative if nobody likes what they create? History's graveyard is full of artists celebrated for being "ahead of their time"—but only retroactively, since they died poor and unappreciated before they could get there. Van Gogh made no money from his paintings, and even Bach's music was dismissed as being "over-elaborate and old fashioned" during his lifetime (8).

But if the public is the ultimate judge of creative value, how do you calculate the fleeting impact of fads? Or of influential critics who get excited about something that puts everyone else to sleep (and vice versa)? Many times in my two decades of jazz writing, a colleague's review has made me wonder if we heard the same music. Then there's the frequent disconnect between critical praise and public favor that can churn up great stress in a creative life. One famous example is Stephen Sondheim's musical *Follies*, which won seven Tony Awards in 1971 but lost its entire investment ($800,000) because of poor attendance.

"Originality" is yet another lump in the sauce. While newness seems central to the concept of creativity, by itself it guarantees neither admiration nor acceptance. In an ingenious study, Simonton fed 15,618 classical melodies into a computer that evaluated the originality of their first six notes. When he plotted the results against the frequency of performance, he discovered that the most original pieces were not the most popular. The favorite music actually sat somewhere between "hackneyed" and "aggravating," nestled in the sweet spot between familiar and boring (9).

Even if you doubt that six notes are enough to evaluate originality, and dismiss the musical judgment of computers, this study was a bold attempt to hoist something quantifiable out of the creative morass. I can also offer some anecdotal support for the idea that a mix of the known and the new is most appealing. In the song "Don't Know Why," the monster debut for singer Norah Jones in 2002, the first five notes are identical to those of Vince Guaraldi's beloved "Charlie Brown's Christmas" and lead right into an unmistakable quote from

Paul McCartney's "Yesterday." These subliminal echoes of cherished anthems helped propel the song to number one, providing just enough nostalgia to soothe the listener without waking the beast of copyright infringement.

"Talent" is yet another concept that's easier to recognize than define. At least "productivity" has tangible units of measurement, but it's more relevant in business than art—after all, it only took a handful of stories to vault Franz Kafka and J. D. Salinger into the permanent pantheon of great writers.

Even premature death affects creativity by enhancing our view of how great someone *might* have been. Jazz has a long list of such tragic icons, including saxophonist Charlie "Bird" Parker and bassist Paul Chambers, both of whom died at thirty-four, and bassist Jaco Pastorius, whose stormy life ended at thirty-six. Their brilliance is undisputed, but their legends—like those of Judy Garland, James Dean, Otis Redding, and Heath Ledger—draw additional voltage from our communal sense of bafflement and loss.

Today creativity has come to encompass so much that it hardly means anything at all. In the ivory tower, whole careers are built on identifying its components and their interactions, and there are many excellent books to explore for those who want to wade further in. But it's also possible to detour around the confusion by leaving creativity undefined.

Now and then writers are so impatient with square one that they leap right over it, and nobody seems to mind. Researchers have made real scientific progress in understanding creativity without even mentioning the concept—as when mapping the brains of people playing music, which is described in chapter 7.

Big Bad C

FOR ALL THE hoopla about cultivating creativity, it also has a negative side, even when it falls short of genius level. Psychologist Hans Eysenck puts it this way:

Creativity, solemnly praised, is in fact anathema. It threatens
the structure and cannot be tolerated—the creative person is
willy nilly turned into a rebel, an outcast, a maverick [. . . or
diagnosed as bipolar?]. (10)

Although creativity can be a kind of life-enhancing filigree, like a
gift for languages or a knack for soufflés, turning it into a livelihood is
something else altogether. Many parents who value creativity mistrust
the creative life, recognizing the vast difference between funding their
future lawyer's sax lessons and coaxing her into a jazz career. But this
paradox is easily resolved by a gesture worthy of Solomon: whacking
creativity into two types, the ordinary (little c) and the great (Big C).

Popular for more than six decades, this distinction separates the
cozy creativity—the domesticated companion who solves daily problems and tosses off witty remarks—from the scary kind, the mystical
midwife of humanity's greatest art and ideas. Unlike little c, which is
a universal plug-in, Big C requires a specific human vessel in which
to flourish; it is sadistically elusive, despite the most urgent of invita-
tions. It is also where the greatest madness supposedly lies.

Much of the Big C research has focused on people who are considered "eminent," which presumes that public acclaim comes only to
the talented (for an alternate view, see Hilton, Paris, and Kardashians,
Any). Some scholars file all their subjects in the same drawer, despite
the obvious differences in achievements and domains. For example, in
Arnold Ludwig's widely cited *The Price of Greatness* (1995), the same
factors that elevated Ernest Hemingway and George Gershwin in
their respective fields are supposed to boost Henry Ford, Albert Einstein, and Martin Luther King in theirs. This seems reductionistic,
at best. As psychiatrist William Frosch suggests in his discussion of
creativity research,

The impulse to create and the skills necessary to each of the tasks
are likely to differ. It may be that we are linking many kinds of

acts because they are special and mystifying, not because they are the same. (11)

Big C was a major interest for Freud, who painted it with his usual limited palette of depression and discontent. His philosophy was basically this: once parents pour your mold and it sets, life becomes a constant struggle against its (always) uncomfortable fit. And so the very best that people can expect, even those who faithfully undergo the treatment he invented, is to replace their aberrant "hysterical misery" with the "common unhappiness" suffered by everyone else. In a universe that runs on pain, Freud reduces creativity to a consolation prize for the frustrated:

> [The artist] is one who is urged on by instinctual needs which are too clamorous; he longs to attain honour, power, riches, fame, and the love of women; but he lacks the means for achieving these gratifications. So, like any other with an unsatisfied longing, he turns away from reality and transfers all his interest, and his libido [sex drive] too, on to the creation of his wishes in the life of phantasy . . . every hungry soul looks to it for comfort and consolation. (12)

Even the creative explorations of Leonardo da Vinci, whom Freud greatly admired, were propelled by his frustrated homosexuality: "He has investigated instead of loving," said Sigmund, who would know about that, reportedly giving up sex himself at the age of forty-one (13). Freud's views deserve more than this drive-by mention, so he will surface again in chapter 4.

In any event, whenever the tired old notion of creative personality drags itself along, there are all kinds of rusty clichés clanking behind it. At best, Big C people are moody, self-centered, high-strung, and unreliable; at worst, they are wildly emotional and teeter on the verge of psychosis and suicidal despair. Or they're absent-minded buffoons, since people with their heads in the clouds tend to stumble over things on the ground. Even the great cultural sage Ann Landers weighed in on this one, suggesting that "all families should have three children; in case one turns out to be a genius, there will be two others to support him" (14).

People who buy this whole piñata are convinced that Big C's hover so close to meltdown that they desperately lunge at poetry or music just to vent their emotional pressure cookers. For some, art is the mental prophylactic that prevents dangerous leakage; for others, it's a buildup that must be released: "If I don't write to empty my mind, I go mad," said Byron, in his usual understated way (15). He would surely appreciate the French poet and playwright Antonin Artaud's take on it:

> There is in every madman a misunderstood genius, whose idea, shining in his head, frightened people, and for whom delirium is the only solution to the strangulation that life had prepared for him. (16)

Such effusions are seen as solid empirical proof for those who believe in creative fragility, since the myth dictates that Big C's are either inflamed by mania, frozen in despair, or endlessly whiplashed between the two. But it's just as easy—and much better documented—to view the creative process as healthy and life-affirming. In fact,

> psychological studies have shown again and again that, however much we want to romanticize [genius], it is typified by qualities that are disappointingly opposite of psychotic: self-discipline, tenacity, organization, calmness, and strong self-image. (17)

There is extensive research to support this positive view and bring the genius out of the shadows. Here comes some of the best.

The Sunny Side

HARVARD PSYCHIATRIST ALBERT Rothenberg and his team conducted a great deal of the authoritative research on the creative mind. Rather than making athletic inferential leaps from centuries of gossip, they gathered firsthand data from people they could speak to without a Ouija board. These were living artists and scientists who had won prestigious awards, such as the Nobel and Pulitzer Prizes, National Gold Medal and Poet Laureate designations, or had been elected to such elite organizations as the National Academy of Sciences and the Royal Academy of London.

The achievers were interviewed at different stages of their creative projects—from the initial idea to its ultimate realization—in order to shed light on the process. Rothenberg's team also spoke to family members and conducted controlled psychological experiments that were designed to identify characteristic creative thinking. After *twenty-five* years of this, they concluded that

> first, contrary to popular as well as professional belief, there is no specific personality type associated with outstanding creativity. Creative people are not necessarily childish and erratic in human relationships, as is often thought, nor are they necessarily extraordinarily egotistic or rebellious or eccentric.

And here's the kicker:

> Only one characteristic of personality and orientation to life and work is absolutely across the board, present in ALL creative people: motivation. They want specifically to create and be creative, [which requires] direct, intense, and intentional effort. (18)

Unfortunately, hard work will never be as thrilling as drowning, whether in the white waters of ecstasy or the sludge of despair. This helps explain why Rothenberg's crucial work is only a small, dry footnote in a world full of frenetic splashing.

Also on creativity's hopeful side is the experience of "flow," that delicious moment when ability and challenge are perfectly balanced to produce an exhilarating rush of mastery. (Athletes know it as "being in the zone.") Similar to psychologist Abraham Maslow's notion of "peak experiences," flow also resembles the joyful ecstasy of successful creative inspiration.

Flow was popularized by psychologist Mihaly Csikszentmihalyi, who comes from a uniquely positive perspective. Having survived the Holocaust, he became interested in how people find meaning and happiness in life, not how they cope with their misery. Flow has nothing to do with psychopathology—it's just the opposite, providing the serene timelessness that many seek through yoga and other meditative practices. And while flow is theoretically accessible to everyone, it seems that the greater openness and flexibility of creatives enable them to get there more easily and more often (19).

Psychiatrist and pianist Denny Zeitlin refers to this feeling as "the purity of the merger state," which is "the prerequisite for true creativity"; and speaking of mergers, vocalist Sara Krieger calls it "having sex with music" (20). Pianist Monty Alexander uses "chasing the moment" to describe the ongoing pursuit of this bliss, which makes the hassles and heartbreaks of the music business disappear, at least while it's happening.

The World Out There

Now the searchlight leaves the creative mind to illuminate the environmental influences around it. There's no guarantee that a fortunate setting will spark creativity—or that a barren one will quash it. But adding social variables to the mix is more realistic than treating creatives as if they lived in bubbles, propelled only by their own quirkiness and a splash or two from the family gene pool.

Many researchers have wondered how various aspects of the real world impinge on the creative person. One ongoing debate is whether creativity is a delicate thing, requiring a kind of hothouse nurturing to bloom, or if it's essentially hardy and resilient, able to thrive despite environmental obstacles and personal adversity (21). As with most of these arguments, there are strong points to be made on both sides.

Either way, it's undeniably useful to have someone run interference for people who are trying to create, taking care of external concerns on their behalf (22). There's a common perception that no one can be exceptionally artistic and good at business at the same time, as if these skills are mutually exclusive (many use a simplistic right- versus left-brain dichotomy for this one). However, the notion that creatives are constitutionally incapable of taking out the garbage and showing up on time may well have originated with the creatives themselves (for their own reasons, see "The Bohemian Excuse" in chapter 8.)

There is a long list of environmental factors to consider, including childhood exposure to a creative domain, type and duration of training and support (or lack thereof), and the relative power of assorted incentives and rewards. Early parental loss keeps showing up in artistic biographies; so do firstborn or only children, although the implications of birth order are still being argued. What is clear is that the right mentor can launch the right trainee into the orbit of genius. I've often wondered what Stephen Sondheim might have been if he hadn't grown up so close to the great songwriter Oscar Hammerstein (and so, repeatedly, has he).

Other variables that have been examined include the impact of class (23), culture (24), and color (25). There's also the famous "Ten-Year Rule," which predicts that creative people need a full decade of experience, exposure, and skill acquisition before they can begin to make lasting contributions to their field. This was supported by a study of seventy-six composers that calculated the time between their first musical instruction and their first masterwork. Out of five hundred notable compositions produced by this sample, only three were composed before year 10 of the composer's career (and these were in years 8 and 9) (26).

Despite the classic image of the self-contained genius, common sense dictates that the environment has a powerful impact. As far back as the 1950s, humanistic psychologist Carl Rogers noted that creativity blooms best when people feel psychologically safe and free. Researchers have also identified specific creativity "killers," like the quest for external reward and competition—being judged in relation to others—which encourages people to "play it safe" (27).

Teresa Amabile, author of *Creativity in Context* (1996), is a pioneer of this reality-based approach. An MBA and professor at Harvard Business School, Amabile has always taken a refreshingly pragmatic and nonpathological view of creativity. In her study of what she calls "creativity in the wild," Amabile and her team analyzed 12,000 journal entries by over two hundred people who were doing creative projects at work. They found that creativity is clearly connected to joy and love, and negatively associated with anger, fear, and anxiety—and the evidence, Amabile reports, is "consistent" (28). (That small whirring sound you hear is Freud, spinning in his grave.)

Here's more good news about creative people: they are actually complicated, not crazy; they are disciplined and committed, happy to take on hard projects and work hard at them; and they are intensely focused, with a "rage to master" their chosen domain (29). Amabile suggests that this "passionate craft of creativity"—the discipline and perseverance—is at least as important as talent (30). But she also notes that "scholars' understanding of the creative process and the factors influencing it is still quite limited" (31). And she's not even touching on Big C.

Low-Hanging Fruit

ONE WAY TO demystify the whole process is to pull creativity down from the stars and designate it as an ordinary thing that's accessible to anyone who wants to learn and practice it. Equal opportunity is the promise of the genius-making industry that peddles recipes from eager self-help gurus (*The Genius in All of Us*) as well as books by accomplished artists like choreographer Twyla Tharp (2003). You can even buy *How to Think Like Leonardo: Seven Steps to Genius Every Day*, although you could probably step for many years without coming any closer (32).

The commercializing of creativity undermines its position as an objective, legitimate research question. This has already been "tainted" by its mystical beginnings—all those divine visitations and fluttering Muses—which can make it appear too frivolous for serious scientific study (33). Here's what psychologist Howard Gardner says about the "nonsense" that is marketed to the public about the ease of acquiring creativity:

> "Come for a weekend, learn to brainstorm, learn to free-associate, we'll make you a creative individual." That just doesn't work. It's a serious business for serious people. Creative work requires, I think, being a certain kind of person, which includes being able to work on things for years, a drive not likely to come to people who paid five hundred dollars for a weekend under a tent. (34)

In any event, given the jumble of variables and viewpoints high and low, it's impossible to construct a universal concept of creativity, let alone pinpoint its precise connection to anything else—particularly madness, which also changes shape depending on who's describing it. It's like trying to lasso a cloud.

Creativity and the Musical Mind

SOME FREUDY-CATS (sorry, irresistible) have applied his gloomy principles to music. Psychiatrist Anthony Storr declared that "Freud was right in supposing that [creativity] originates in dissatisfaction." Equating music with self-medication, Storr considers it the perfect refuge for people who don't like people:

> Being the most abstract of the arts, and the least obviously connected directly with human experience, [music] is often

the passion of schizoid people, who delight in discovering that
there is a way of experiencing and expressing emotion which
is impersonal. (35)

Yet even these emotions can be dangerous, especially when listening alone, since they might lead to "a loss of self-identity" (36). Although Freud admitted that explaining creativity was beyond him—
"psychoanalysis can do nothing toward elucidating the nature of the
artistic gift" (37)—that doesn't keep his fans from squinting at it
through his myopic and grimy lens.

Sometimes this psychoanalytic approach gets downright silly—
like the notion that the wistful minor key has something to do with
oral dependency—thumb-sucking, perhaps (38). Then there's the bizarre claim that the minor triad evokes sadness because lowering the
middle note to create it "clearly represents the castration complex,
and hence arouses feelings of anxiety" (39). Since no one explained
how this dynamic applies to women, we can only assume they must
be worried for their men.

Most Big C researchers wander in the territory of writers, because
their GPS rarely includes musical psyches. For one thing, the invisible nature of their art makes its creative process harder to track; for
another, as Frank Zappa famously said, "Talking about music is like
dancing about architecture." But if its message could be verbalized, it
would destroy its uniqueness and defeat its purpose. There's even recent
evidence that talking about music can diminish one's memory of it (40).

Because writers provide the best quotes about their moods and behaviors, they tend to dominate the inquiries into Big C. When musicians want to reveal something personal, they do it in a language that
science doesn't speak. Composers Leonard Bernstein, Aaron Copland,
and Mickey Hart all wrote excellent books about music, but in general musicians are conspicuously absent from discussions of creativity
and madness—unless, centuries after death, someone has gathered up
their life bits into "evidence" of how crazy they were.

The most famous exception is composer Robert Schumann, whose

leap into the Rhine and asylum death two years later were both recorded at the time. What remains in dispute is the cause. As usual,
bipolar disorder is the default diagnosis, but newly translated medical
records suggest late stage syphilis instead, which can produce bizarre
and delusional behavior for a full twenty years before it causes death
(41). There will be further discussion of Schumann and the pox as we
proceed.

Reports from the Front

THE ABOVE COMPARISON of writers and musicians is not just theoretical.
In my own hobnobbing with such creative folk, I've never met a writer
who hesitated to discuss inspiration—most are happy to expound on
it in some detail and at considerable length. In contrast, many musicians are reluctant to say anything at all, as if analyzing their talent
would somehow make it disappear. One composer calls it "meddling
with a natural function":

> There is prevalent the superstition that if a composer devotes
> too much attention to the analysis of the creative process, a ca-
> tastrophe results in which his inspiration is destroyed and his
> art rendered meaningless. (42)

Such hesitation makes musicians useless to researchers who are
seeking dramatic affirmations of madness. This would not surprise
Carl Seashore, the first music psychologist, who wrote that "the normal musical mind is first of all a normal mind" over seven decades
ago (43). More recently, Anthony Kemp observes that musicians are
simply more independent and introverted than the average person
(44). But then Kemp is a musician as well as a psychologist, a combination that offers a unique advantage. As Seashore (also an organist
and choir director) explains it,

While the cold details of musical facts can be recorded and

organized by **a mere psychologist,** validity and interpretation depend upon an intimate knowledge of music and feeling for it. (45, amused emphasis mine)

Unfortunately, this background doesn't always guarantee superior understanding: psychologist Geoffrey Wills was a drummer and still jumped on the "all beboppers are crazy" train (46). You can read about our resulting tango in the *British Journal of Psychiatry* in chapter 5.

Meanwhile, Kemp explains how musicians may feel isolated from a world busy with facts and objects: "Their job is to play upon feeling, to appreciate, to interpret, and to create the beautiful." Some manage their exile with a superior pose, emphasizing their role as "keeper and master of great artistic truths" (47). This outsider attitude becomes a popular shelter for both creatives and those who want to look like them. This too will be described later on.

Understanding musician psychology is difficult when there are more psychology books about the cognitive processing of music than about the people who make it (48); there was no anthology about musical emotion until several generations after Seashore pioneered the field. That book suffers from the same problem as creativity: lack of clear definition and measurement. But at least it says nothing about inherent creative pathology, and has just one reference to depression: "music as treatment of" (49). Refreshing.

Aaron Copland is one of the great musicians who provided useful reports from the front. Although undeniably a Big C, Copland spent little time bemoaning its burdens; instead, he considered creativity to be a valuable tool for self-knowledge, since it helped "make evident one's deepest feelings about life":

But why is the job never done? Why must one always begin again? . . . I must create in order to know myself, and since self-knowledge is a never-ending search, each new work is only a part-answer to the question "Who am I?" and brings with it the need to go on to other and different part-answers. (50)

Such confessional disclosure abounds in autobiographies and interviews, but is hard to find in academic writings. In 2002, when I created a university course in the psychology of music, I found that the textbooks were more focused on the laboratory processing of musical snippets than on how people listen in real life. So I gathered up some of my own publications into a collection called *Thought Food: Readings in the Psychology of Music* and used that, along with the one text that offered a whole section on "real world applications" (51). This was a rare find.

Faces in a Cloud

CONSTRUCTING PSYCHOLOGICAL THEORY can be just as subjective as lying on your back in a summer meadow and finding faces in the shifting shapes above. It's a widely accepted principle that in order to make sense out of ambiguous stimuli, people must dip into their private mental vaults, using their own experiences to project meaning where none exists.

This is the rationale behind the Rorschach (ink blot) test and other such "projective" measures. Because the images you perceive are constructed from pieces of yourself, they can reveal deep truths about what makes you tick—revelations that emerge without your awareness or permission, and may even be news to you. This principle applies to all humans, even the most venerated of psychologists, and helps explain why virtually every theory sits on a subjective foundation.

The brilliant *Faces in a Cloud* (1979) demonstrates how this works with four of the founding fathers: Sigmund Freud, Carl Jung, Wilhelm Reich, and Otto Rank. Comparing their writing to their personal histories, the authors show how these so-called universal theories were actually invented to explain their own lives:

No theorist offers definitive statements on the meaning of being human unless he feels those statements constitute a framework within which he can comprehend his own experience. (52)

This applies to creativity theories too, especially since they contain more debate than data. The truth is that, apart from the neuroscientists who can directly image the brain, every psychological doctrine springs from its author's perspective, and its continued health depends on successful consensus and defense (the process is virtually Talmudic).

For example, when Anthony Storr died, the *U.K. Independent* and the *New York Times* described him as being depressed from an early age. "He was no stranger to suffering," wrote Christopher Lehman-Haupt, blaming the fact that his parents were first cousins (53). But whatever the source of his own pain, Storr projects it onto creatives by painting them as desperate people who cling to art for their emotional salvation. Those were the faces he saw in the cloud, and those were the theories that informed his books, influencing both the public and professional views of creativity.

Similarly, psychologist Alfred Adler invented "the inferiority complex" to explain his childhood misery as the sickly brother of a star athlete; not surprisingly, Adler claimed that people produce art and music "out of their own inadequacies, much as an oyster reacts to the irritation of sand by producing a pearl" (54).

It's easy to see why subjectivity drives the research engine: you do need a strong personal investment to dedicate your life to one particular area. I first learned this during my PhD studies, when the time came to pick a dissertation topic. Knowing that years of slog and sacrifice lay ahead, we all went for something with powerful private resonance, hoping this would carry us through.

My friend Charlie, the Star Trek fan who glued on Spock ears every Halloween, decided to study the shared time perception between therapist and client and how it "warps" as treatment continues. Mark had recently welcomed his first child, so he chose fatherhood. I tested whether musicians' preference for improvisation also shows in the rest of their lives (short answer: pretty much), while another alumna who became a famous sexpert spent her time on inorgasmic women. (Draw your own conclusions.)

The same challenge applies after graduation in choosing academic careers. I know that many creativity researchers are habitual dabblers in the stuff—either accomplished or wannabe painters and pianists, playwrights, and assemblers of collages. Sometimes the link is clear, as when psychologist Ruth Richards, editor of *Everyday Creativity*, describes herself on the book jacket as someone who "draws, writes, and plays three instruments badly" (55). It doesn't take a psychic to understand why Richards studies the kind of creativity that's accessible to everyone. And given that no creative goes home without a diagnosis, little c's get little "mental illnesses" like cyclothymia, a mild cycling of ups and downs that used to be called "moody" (56).

One last observation on the link between professionals and their theories. I have noticed that most of the experts who regularly pass along the mad genius doctrine—and with so little attention to its flaws—are not psychotherapists. With doctorates in social or educational psychology, and careers spent in academic rather than clinical settings, they miss out on the regular, intimate revelations of living creative people.

As such, they may lack firsthand knowledge of what these people are actually tackling, and what they themselves view as their primary problems. In addition, as theorists and not therapists, these academics do not witness, assist in, or clinically evaluate the many solutions that creatives may attempt. Please note: this lack of experience doesn't imply any lack of sincerity or compassion. But the fact is that supporting and guiding graduate students, however kindly or effectively, will never be the same thing as engaging in psychotherapy, with its unique depth of connection and insight.

Moreover, without such ongoing, intimate encounters, it's likely that these scholars are less familiar with the myriad daily repercussions of a bipolar diagnosis. For some, it's even possible—dare I say it?—that Big C people are not quite real: they are abstractions, impersonal and remote. This makes it easier to toss serious psychiatric labels around and consign the genius to a lifetime of serious pathology. Certainly, their guessing from a distance could make them tone-deaf to the quiet creative struggles in real life, and more susceptible to the hyperbolic claims of the flamboyant.

The Non-Theory Theories

A FINAL WORD on defining creativity (or the impossibility of doing so) comes from psychologist Sigmund Koch, one of the pioneers of this research. From the early 1980s to the mid-1990s, as director of the Boston University Aesthetics Research Project, Koch conducted intensive conversations with eminent artists; alas for us, this work generated no published studies.

But while interviewing the celebrated playwright Arthur Miller, Koch was able to expound on his doubt that creativity will ever be fully understood:

> We're in a scientistic society . . . that presumes you can find some kind of simplistic, or in some sense, complete explanation of everything. There are still many people in my field . . . who would tend to think in these terms: why shouldn't a theory of creativity be possible? This is gibberish. It's very important to establish exactly the senses and the boundaries in which one has simply to stand in awe of the ineffable. (57)

There are almost as many definitions as there are definers. Well, here's mine: I believe that creativity is too individualized for any one-size-fits-all packaging, no matter how logical, just as no single explanation covers anything else that humans aspire to, enjoy, or suffer. Of course, this never discourages psychologists from trying to find one, and the chances are excellent that they will stay on this quest as well.

It's not out of the question that psychic pain can increase the depth to an artist's work, adding wisdom and empathy to her perspective. But is true madness really a prerequisite for great art? And how will we ever know for sure? Here's a radical thought: perhaps we don't need to. It's a safe bet that however it works, creative people will keep producing things that others cannot, despite every attempt to demystify the process and capture its magic with words. It's even possible that explaining it will destroy it; as Leonard Bernstein wrote,

> Please, God, leave us this one mystery, unsolved: why man creates. The minute that one is solved, I fear art will cease to be. (58)

And so the searchlight glides past creativity to the next mystery. As we will see, "madness" is every bit as hard to define as "creativity." Unfortunately, the stakes are much higher.

TWO

Elastic Madness

One Size Fits All

If you cut a thing up, of course it will smell. Hence nothing raises such an infernal stink as human psychology.

~ *D. H. Lawrence*

CENTURIES AGO, WHEN THE NOTION of "mental illness" first arrived, there were only rumors about where and how this supposed
"disease" process took place. Not a surprise, given the rudimentary tools
of the time. But today, even with our high-tech measurement devices,
we still can't verify what occurs in cells that are one-hundredth the
size of a decimal point and conduct their mysterious business at two
hundred times a second (1).

Despite the widespread use of the term "mental illness," science has
yet to satisfy three criteria that would make it a valid medical entity:

1. Specific, readily identifiable diseased tissue

2. Dependable chemical tests

3. Reasonably accurate prognoses

It doesn't help when people with the same diagnosis have very
different courses and outcomes, and medications that help some are

quite useless for others. The variability is so extensive that it's hard to believe there's any kind of unitary "disease" process at work—and nothing has reliably emerged after decades of searching.

In the meantime, the DSM can only offer an assortment of theoretical categories and labels for every human quirk (with more riding in on every revision). Since it's just a collection of perceived behaviors—descriptions of what disorders are supposed to look like—the diagnostic process is highly vulnerable to subjective value judgments and agendas. But because it constitutes a common language for discussing problematic behavior, it is used worldwide by mental health professionals, patients, scientists, health care agencies, hospitals, pharmaceutical and insurance companies, social services, school systems, universities, courts, and prisons. This gargantuan influence is often equated with truth—especially since there's nothing to compare or compete with it.

Because We Say So

Officially, the DSM does not presume to describe illnesses, yet terminology like "symptoms," "remission," and "clinical" gives it a distinctly medical whiff and weight. Moreover, it presents its categories as if they were just as real as a heart attack.

But heart attacks don't require negotiation to exist. In contrast, mental disorders are hammered out by backstage arguments full of intra-guild squabbling and self-interested trading (I'll support your new disorder if you'll vote for mine), and—all too often—corruption. At one recent point, every expert working on the depression category had financial ties to the pharmaceutical industry (2).

Although the DSM criteria might be amorphous, they define legitimate mental disorders because—well, because psychiatry says they do. That's how "jet lag" became a mental disorder (it's coded 307.45, on page 578).

To blur things even further, making a diagnosis requires choosing from a menu of possibilities, such as "three of the following seven symptoms," which must also occur "often," although the DSM never specifies exactly what that means. Weekly? Daily? Three times an hour? One thing is certain: the more beleaguered the witness, the more often the annoying behavior will seem to occur. In fact, more than 90 percent of childhood diagnoses are based only on the parents' description of their offspring, with no reference to any other observer or context (3).

DSM categories are also imprecise because so many of the symptoms are implicit in one another. For example, speaking of beleaguered witnesses, take ADHD, a common label for unruly children, especially boys. Currently it requires the child to exhibit—often—at least six of the following nine behaviors:

1. Does not seem to listen

2. Does not follow through on instructions

3. Has difficulty organizing tasks

4. Loses things

5. Is easily distracted

6. Fails to pay close attention

7. Has difficulty sustaining attention

8. Is forgetful

9. Avoids or dislikes homework (4)

It's obvious that many of these behaviors overlap, making it easy to rack up the number needed for diagnosis. For instance, disorganized children are more likely to lose things, and kids who can't or won't pay attention will be predictably disinclined to do homework. But is this cumulative evidence of a disorder, or just a paraphrase of its most obvious signs? And how different are "failing to pay" attention and "having difficulty sustaining" it, anyway?

Follow the Money

WHEN THE FIRST DSM was adapted from a military manual and published in 1952 by the APA, it had sixty categories of mental disorders. The latest major edition—the DSM-IV—arrived in 2000 packing 374. For the DSM-5, due in May of 2013, the traditional Roman numeral has been dropped to facilitate "incremental updates"—in other words, new interim editions can be easily identified as DSM-5.1, 5.2 and so on, forcing consumers to keep paying for updates. It's well-known that a major portion of the APA's income comes from DSM sales, with another 25 percent provided by drug company ads in their various journals (5).

Then there are the individual benefits. Most of the recent 4,000 percent increase in pediatric bipolar diagnoses has been traced back to the go-to psychiatrist on the disorder (Dr. Joseph Biederman), who received $1.4 million from the drug makers but neglected to report it to the government—which happened to be paying him handsomely to objectively evaluate those same drugs (6).

Yet the problem is hardly restricted to one individual: between 1996 and 2004, advertising helped increase U.S. bipolar diagnoses nearly 300 percent for adolescents and over 400 percent for children. Many of these labels were "upcoded" from lesser conditions to jump the ever-higher insurance barriers blocking reimbursement and inpatient care.

After decades of watching such things unfold, I can't help launching into a diatribe, particularly when the public is fed such an egregious bunch of horse . . . radish. Note, for instance, *Time* magazine's "Is Your Child Bipolar?" worksheet, first printed in 2002 and available online for nine years: if parents can check twenty "warning signs" out of forty-one, they should hustle their child to a professional evaluation.

According to this document, alarming behaviors include being "very intuitive or very creative" and having "many ideas at once." "Poor handwriting" is also on the list, which qualifies most of the people I know. With this kind of widely disseminated information, is it any wonder that the public is so confused about the nature and prevalence of psychiatric disorders—and so vulnerable to authoritative pronouncements (7)?

There are strong disagreements within the field as well. In 2010, psychiatrist Allen J. Frances, who chaired the DSM-IV task force, pointed out that even their careful field trials "completely failed to predict the later false epidemics in attention deficit, bipolar, and autistic disorder." He also noted that the DSM-5 includes many new diagnoses at the threshold of normality that "have the potential to reclassify as mentally disordered tens of millions of people currently considered normal."

Frances sees the new manual as "an unhappy combination of soaring ambition and remarkably weak methodology" (8). Psychiatrist Steven E. Hyman, a member of the current DSM-5 Task Force, criticizes the classification system as "scientifically immature," with its diagnoses merely "placeholders pending advances in research" (9). But this is not how it's presented to the world.

Because of such ongoing turf battles as well as the perennial need for more customers, DSM categories tend to morph and expand with every revision. The classic *Making Us Crazy* documents precisely the kind of jabberwocky that clause 6 of the APA's work agreement was intended to obscure. This book provides a fascinating look at the process by which psychiatric disorders "multiply like guppies," and are then imposed on the public through a worldwide campaign of communal gaslighting. In her writings, psychologist Paula J. Caplan describes her close encounters with the DSM decision-making process and the wide variety of harm caused by such unscientific diagnoses (10).

OK, You Caught Us

OFFICIALLY, THE APA has long denied the blatant influence of politics and profits on DSM categories. But in 2003, six "psychiatric survivors" (former mental patients) forced them to show their hand. Declaring a hunger strike—the Fast for Freedom in Mental Health—they demanded proof that emotional distress is caused by known diseases and/or chemical imbalances in the brain that can be identified by laboratory tests.

After twenty-one days, the APA capitulated and issued their "Statement on Diagnosis and Treatment of Mental Disorders," publicly conceding—in writing—that they couldn't point to any definite biological basis for the disorders they were selling.

But they also quickly mobilized the classic squid defense: blasting out clouds of ink to confuse the enemy and obscure the issue. The statement goes on to praise "the tremendous investment of the Nation" (yes, capitalized—you can almost hear the marching band) in understanding "severe mental and behavior disorders." In a dazzling spin worthy of *Dancing with the Stars*, the press release proceeds to scold those who "persist in questioning" psychiatry, while simultaneously excusing their own confusion because "the brain is the most complex and challenging object of study in the history of human science." In other words, they may not know everything, but they will *not* be doubted.

Still, the APA surrendered enough ground to get the strikers eating again when they admitted that

> brain science has not advanced to the point where scientists or clinicians can point to readily discernible pathologic lesions or genetic abnormalities that in and of themselves serve as reliable or predictive biomarkers of a given mental disorder or mental disorders as a group. (11)

When the APA provided no evidence of bona fide illnesses—even when publicly backed against the wall—they confirmed that psychiatry is more speculation than science, despite the "Science Based" claim on their masthead. But rather than dwell on this embarrassment, the press release quickly shifts the focus to "the irrefutable devastating emotional and financial tolls" caused by, well, whatever these things are.

At the end, they wrap the statement in the flag, promising to "strive to achieve the President's New Freedom Mental Health vision" (which included the Big Brother-ish idea, since abandoned, to perform mass mental health "screenings" on all preschool and school-age children in the United States). Finally, with one last inky squirt, the APA vows "not to be distracted by those who would deny that serious mental disorders are real medical conditions that can be diagnosed accurately and treated effectively" (12).

To be fair, this problem is not confined to psychiatry alone. In 2009, some psychologists caused a considerable uproar about the lack of science in their own clinical practice, calling it "an unconscionable embarrassment for many reasons" (13). They claimed that too many practitioners were ignoring empirical advances in technique and methodologies, preferring to use whatever "felt good" to them instead. This complaint originated in-house but quickly appeared in *Newsweek* under the screaming headline "Why Do Psychologists Reject Science?" (14).

Getting Skewed

Despite the foregoing evidence to the contrary, let's assume for a giddy moment that the DSM really does describe valid and verifiable biological entities. But it still has a serious reliability problem, because even when professionals use the same guidelines, diagnostic agreement has never been perfect—or even very high. In five controlled studies, the very best rate of agreement among psychiatrists was 63 percent and the worst 10 percent—although considering the DSM's fuzziness, this comes as no surprise (15).

It's easy for bias to skew the results when a process is so intangible. Discrimination also slithers into the mix, as when clinicians judge lower-class patients as more disordered than others, find more schizophrenia in blacks than whites, and evaluate women as being more disturbed than men, despite their identical symptoms (16).

There's more. A study of sixty psychologists and psychiatrists demonstrated that personal theories play a significant role (those clouds and faces again). And given the option, practitioners often choose personal beliefs over any empirical findings, considering them to be "the real or moral truth" (17). There may be memory distortions as well: once clinicians settled on a diagnosis, even if the patient showed none of its most important symptoms, the clinicians remembered that they did (18). Surprisingly, training and experience can make little difference in assessment ability:

> Studies show that professionals often fail to reach reliable or valid conclusions and that the accuracy of their judgments does not necessarily surpass that of laypersons, thus raising substantial doubts that psychologists or psychiatrists meet legal standards for expertise. (19)

Because the mood disorder category embraces normal ups and downs as well as more immobilizing conditions, virtually everyone can get a seat at that table (and there's the mad genius over there, right behind the pickle tray). Of all the pathologies, mood diagnoses are the easiest to expand, and given their expensive treatments, there are tempting financial incentives for doing so.

The DSM-IV "Mood Disorders" section contains all possible combinations and shades of depression and mania, from the Big Problems (Major Depression, Bipolar I, and Bipolar II) to the less severe (dysthymic and cyclothymic disorders), lifelong habits of slumping or cycling moods that raise few alarms and were once considered merely features of temperament.

There are qualifiers (seasonal? postpartum?) and disqualifiers (rule out thyroid problems, substance abuse), and everything gets a five-digit code for insurance purposes. And, as with virtually every other disorder, the catchall "looks like a duck" category of NOS (Not Otherwise Specified) is available for people who don't quite fit the established criteria but get the diagnosis anyway.

Psychiatrist Hagop Askikal, not coincidentally the director of a mood disorder clinic in California, has proposed some new categories. In addition to Bipolar I and II, there would be I 1/2, II 1/2, III, III 1/2, and IV, and provisions for substance abusers, people over fifty, and those "erroneously" diagnosed with borderline or narcissistic personality disorders. Proposed future coverage includes sociopaths, bulimics, obsessive compulsives, sex addicts, gamblers, and those with sleep complaints (20).

There's no question that much of what gets into the DSM-5 is motivated by self-interest. Some people want more attention paid to their own areas of expertise. Others push for a new specialty that would harness their particular talents, elevate their professional profile, and increase their billable hours. Psychiatry—as well as any other profession that involves caring for people—is not a self-denying religious order. Nor should it be. However, a bit more objectivity and attention to science (or honest admission about the lack of it) would be a good thing.

Moody, Mad, or Just Really Creative?

FORTUNATELY, WE DON'T need to dive into the whole pool of confusion to understand why there's such a stubborn linkage between bipolar disorder and genius. We only need to see how it works in a real-life context.

Let's say you're a jazz musician. According to the DSM-IV, you are experiencing a manic episode if you exhibit any three of the following seven symptoms:

1. Inflated self-esteem

2. Decreased need for sleep

3. More talkative than usual

4. "Flight of ideas" or the experience of racing thoughts

5. Distractibility or difficulty differentiating between the relevant and irrelevant

6. Increased goal-directed activity (either socially, at work, at school, or sexually)

7. Excessive involvement in pleasurable activities having a high potential for painful consequences (21)

Here's how these symptoms could manifest in your daily life:

1. You decide to finally finish your CD, planning to quit your day job once all that money comes rolling in (symptoms 1 and 7).

2. You use every spare moment to work on it (symptom 6), including staying up all night (symptom 2).

3. You allow yourself to free-associate and generate random creative ideas (symptoms 5 and 4).

4. You talk excitedly about it (symptom 3).

5. You feel really confident about the whole thing (back to symptoms 1 and 7).

This scenario, instantly familiar to any creative person with an exciting new project, gives you more than twice as many symptoms as you need.

All that's left is for your "mania" to meet one of the following three conditions:

1. It causes marked impairment in occupational functioning or in usual social activities or relationships with others.

2. It necessitates hospitalization.

3. It has psychotic features.

The first condition is a cinch. "Marked impairment in usual relationships" could simply mean irritating the hell out of friends and family by being so obsessed that you're oblivious to them and their needs. And if you're sleeping on that day job because of all those late nights, you've racked up some serious "occupational impairment" as well.

The other two options (involuntary hospitalization and psychosis) are the most serious. Once the definitive hallmarks of madness, they're no longer required to make the diagnosis. Neither is promiscuity or excessive spending, traditionally the two riskiest behaviors with the worst long-term consequences.

But if you loosen the net, you catch more fish. This also encourages the invention of marginal categories where people acquire the ominous blush of a serious disorder, if not its full coloration, like the "subsyndromal" person who is only a "little bit" manic-depressive and "must struggle on alone, wondering what is the matter with him" (22).

The DSM does have a rigid all-or-nothing tradition—you either have a disorder or you don't, which leaves people who fall just short of the required symptoms in a kind of psychiatric limbo. There are rumors that the new edition will contain a new category of "conditions" that are not serious enough to be disorders but still require treatment; while this makes sense at first, it also opens a Pandora's box full of unnecessary diagnoses that pathologize (and invariably medicate) too many people.

Another controversial proposal in the wind involves labeling serious conditions that are not currently present, but that *may* occur sometime in the future. This is supposed to enable early treatment (again, pharmaceuticals at the ready) and prevent unnecessary suffering. But there are three immediate problems with this premise: it relies on psychiatry's notoriously weak predictive powers, it confers stigma and shame, and it could easily trigger any number of self-fulfilling prophecies. This is called Attenuated Psychotic Symptoms Syndrome, which can be diagnosed even if the evidence is considered "equivocal." Moreover, although the word "risk" appears on the website to describe the disorder, it was excised from its official name—perhaps to avoid the likely firestorm over labeling people who might (operative word: "might") have problems later in life (23).

Creative Pathology versus Creative Reality

As it is today—even before the DSM-5 unveils its new categories—anyone who's ever had a mood can get diagnosed with some mood disorder or other. It's easy for those whose lives center around great creative efforts—those Big C's—especially since so many mental health professionals seem to be unfamiliar with their creative process and the stresses unique to that way of life (see "Welcome to the Stresstival" in chapter 8). It's always simpler to attribute creative behavior to some intrapsychic hullabaloo when real-life challenges are ignored.

A common misconception among mad genius researchers is the notion that creativity is a continuous state, so that any variations in productivity must be caused by some interfering pathology. After all, why would anyone with such a wonderful gift not be using it all the time?

This is the rationale for all those widely disseminated timelines, where the quiet stretches of great artists become "evidence" of their depression, and the spikes in activity are equated with mania. But other explanations are certainly possible.

Here's one: when Aaron Copland was asked why he hadn't written anything lately, he replied that he hadn't gotten any interesting musical ideas (24). This is perfectly reasonable. And given the natural cycle of activity and rest, every field needs time to lie fallow after a bountiful harvest—in the same way, creative people must recharge after their own.

Professionals also distort reality when they focus on the dizzy whirl of inspiration as if it were the defining creative moment. Its intensity can mimic mania, and it's a lot sexier than hard work and diligence. But inspiration is "neither the invariant starting point of the creative process nor necessarily the most critical aspect" (25).

Many people believe in the "incubation" phase, when you stop obsessing over a creative problem, walk away, and let your brain simmer it until it's done. Yet that "aha!" moment is also more complex than it seems: it may be the culmination of a series of events that happen at different times and places in the brain (26).

One reason it's hard to sort this out is that, on paper, the definitions of inspiration and mania overlap so closely that it takes a chart to pry them apart. Fortunately, I made one up years ago, using the official DSM-IV guidelines for mania on page 332:

Comparing Creative and Manic States

Creative	Manic
Distances self from daily stressors in order to concentrate	Distances self from stressors because cannot concentrate
In own world; unique viewpoint	In own world; unique viewpoint
Reduced need for food and sleep	Reduced need for food and sleep
Annoyed when interrupted or challenged	Enraged when interrupted or challenged
Intense, enthused, full of plans	Intense, enthused, full of plans
Need for ongoing self-examination	Trapped in self-absorption
Ideas come fast	Ideas come too fast
Unusual access to unconscious	Overwhelmed by unconscious
After productivity, depletion and recharge	After mania, depression and despair

As the chart demonstrates, the main distinction between normal and the pathological is the element of control—a few notches up this dial, and the picture completely changes. The creative whirlwind typically ends when the product is done, but for the truly manic, the off switch has disappeared beneath an increasingly rapid, delusional avalanche of ideas. People caught in this frenzy lack the filters and judgment to produce masterpieces—their madness obstructs rather than enhances their artistic efforts, no matter what the myth may dictate.

Csikszentmihalyi's "flow," introduced in chapter 1, resembles inspiration, when the artist's self-awareness dissolves into a powerful wave of creative mastery. But those lucky enough to experience this are not helpless, doomed to endless whipsawing between emotional highs and lows. Rather,

> the energy is under their own control—it is not controlled by the calendar [or] the clock . . . They consider the rhythm of activity followed by idleness or reflection very important for the success of their work . . . a strategy for achieving their goals. (27)

This total immersion, sense of timelessness, and inattention to hunger and fatigue are all natural parts of this process; Koch emphasized "concentration to such an extent that the 'self' disappears" (28). Attorney and author Denise Shekerjian interviewed forty MacArthur "genius grant" winners and found that

> in the end, the common themes linking these creative people separated and floated to the surface like cream . . . they were all driven, remarkably resilient, adept at creating an environment that suited their needs, skilled at honoring their own peculiar talents instead of lusting after an illusion of self, capable of knowing when to follow their instincts, and above all, magnificent risk-takers, unafraid to run ahead of the great popular tide. (29)

Also inherent in exceptional creativity is the rare ability to juggle opposing thoughts at the same time: Rothenberg calls it "Janusian thinking," for the Roman god who looks both backwards and ahead, as many of us do in January when resolving to avoid old mistakes (30). Psychiatrists call it Symptom 5 of mania.

Finally, it's good to keep in mind the fundamental logical error of assuming that when someone harbors both great creativity and mental disorder, the two must be intimately related. As you learn in Stat 101, correlation is not causality. Expecting that creativity will always depend on madness is like believing your team keeps winning because you wear the same T-shirt to every game.

An Elephant Is a Submarine

EVEN IF A diagnosis achieves professional consensus, it may be disconnected from reality. To illustrate, let's say that a DSM task force meets, wrangles, breaks for lunch, and by day's end agrees that an elephant will henceforth and forever be called "a submarine." This means that each time someone identifies a pachyderm as a submarine, they can chalk up some "interrater reliability." This was the guiding principle behind the DSM in the first place: to ensure that everyone identifies the same signs of abnormal behavior in the same language. Still, that doesn't turn an elephant into a submarine.

This also applies to labeling a specific creative behavior as "a symptom of bipolar disorder." The more people equate the two, the more they will continue to be equated, thus creating a "reliable" connection. But whether this reflects anything real is another matter altogether: validity is more integral to a concept's value than how many people will buy into it. Put another way: does creative enthusiasm reliably signify pathological behavior in and of itself, or only because professionals have agreed to define it that way?

People can sidestep this pothole by ignoring definitions altogether. This is a popular solution for bypassing such validity concerns according to an extensive survey of creativity measurement (31). The concept of madness has similar conceptual drawbacks, but at least there are direct financial benefits to tiptoeing around those; as sociologist Allan Horwitz argues,

> Because diagnostic psychiatry has little concern for validity . . . current conceptions of mental illness include far more behaviors than a valid definition of disorder warrants. The

consequences . . . are that rates of presumed mental illness are elevated to artificially high levels, [and] non-disordered people are treated as if they are disordered. (32)

Psychiatry already has serious credibility problems and is likely headed for more, given the increased velocity of journalistic exposés as 2013 approaches. Things haven't changed much in the many years since forensic psychiatrist Bernard Diamond wrote this:

The whole profession of psychiatry is so preoccupied with its own omniscience and too unsure in its public status that it is afraid to expose its deficiencies about some of the most fundamental problems of human nature. (33)

To be fair, it doesn't help that the social definitions of abnormality are also constantly changing. In 1851, slaves who tried to run away were said to suffer from the pathological disorder of "drapetomania" (from the Greek "drapetes," or "runaway," and "mania," or frenzy). Would anyone call that a mental disorder now? Throughout history, auditory hallucinations (hearing voices) have been both positively valued and considered a clear sign of madness (34). Similarly, homosexuality was a DSM mental disorder until psychiatry shifted away from that kind of thinking. Today, it's fashionable for young people to attach metal hoops to their tongues and genitalia. We can only guess what earlier clinicians would have made of this.

The mad genius has long wobbled in the wind of guesswork and confusion but has managed to continue its steady march through the ages. Let's see how—and why. Next.

PART TWO

Greeks to Freaks

THREE

Melancholy Becomes Romantic

I have known no man of genius who had not to pay, in
some affliction or defect either physical or spiritual, for
what the gods had given him.

~ *Sir Max Beerbohm*

W HILE BEERBOHM WAS A HUMORIST, he was clearly onto something serious. Like birds, humans often mistrust those who
stand out from the flock. But the choice to act on this difference—
whether to applaud or persecute it, or simply dismiss it with a pejorative label—tends to vary with the cultural mood.

Because the mad genius idea has been around for more than two
thousand years, its defenders point to its longevity as proof of its credibility. But fables can be repeated forever without becoming facts. And
so this myth, like any other folklore, rides the historical pendulum
that swings between excess and retreat: what was forbidden yesterday
will be celebrated tomorrow, just as caution turns into courage and
restraints break loose, allowing freedom out for another run.

Other factors also affect a culture's fondness for its geniuses. History shows that secure and successful societies tend to be open-minded
and generous toward their nonconformists. In contrast, communities
waging war or experiencing social and economic upheaval may act

nervous and suspicious—much like insecure people, they seek refuge in the familiar and purge their anxieties on those who don't fit in.

There's always the chance of projection, that "faces in a cloud" technique that operates whenever people need to explain something ambiguous. And sometimes, it's only the wheel of fashion taking another spin. But whatever the dynamics of a specific time or place, whenever we pan out for the long view, we can see the mad genius moving from sun into shadow, and back again.

This historical survey won't calibrate every switchback, present every expert, or fill every chronological gap. But the overall message is clear: if the mad genius were truly a hard scientific fact, it would never be this vulnerable to society's passing fancies. After all, the existence of gravity doesn't depend on its current popularity.

Lost in Translation

THE WHOLE THING began with gods descending from Mount Olympus to literally "breathe" ("inspire") ideas into a few lucky artists. According to Plato, the poet has to "leave his senses" to create his best work. This sounds like a psychiatric crisis, but in fact, divine inspiration was a productive and yearned-for visitation. Plato even declares, "We should not be afraid of madness," and goes on to describe its four kinds: divine inspiration, love, prophecy, and ecstatic worship.

Plato also points out, "Some of our greatest blessings come from madness, which is given by the gods to help us achieve the greatest happiness" (1). This inspirational "insanity" was so friendly that the Greeks called it "enthousiasmos," the pleasure of "having a god within," which translates as a mild state that needs a modifier to become extreme (as in, "*wild* enthusiasm"). Moreover, this celestial gift was such an honor that creators received no money for anything they wrote under its influence (2), beginning the unfortunate tradition of the underpaid artist who's supposed to live on creative satisfaction alone.

A similar misunderstanding applies to Aristotle's famous contention that "all great men are melancholic." Like Plato's "madness" this is interpreted retroactively, with our modern clinical understanding of the word infusing Aristotle's viewpoint. In his day, the word "melancholic" did not mean depressed, only "possessing black bile." A central concept in early Greek medicine, black bile is one of the four "humors," vital saps that flow through the body affecting behavior and moods (the others are blood, phlegm, and yellow bile). A serious imbalance of these fluids was thought to cause disease, but a bit more of one only affected temperament.

For Aristotle, the melancholic temperament provided the ideal launching pad for genius. He describes an optimal melancholic state— a kind of Goldilocks compromise in which the black bile is neither too hot nor too cold, but just right. In his *Problemata*, he explains that these lucky melancholics "have more practical wisdom and **are less eccentric** and in many respects superior to others either in education or in the arts or in public life" (3, emphasis mine).

It is best to be in the center position, Aristotle says, where it's easier to access both free imagination and realistic appraisal. Despite this image of alternating between opposites, this was not bipolar disorder, or anything like it—it was only the fortunate capacity to integrate two complimentary functions.

Fast-forward to the 1980s, when this same idea resurfaces in all the right/left brain hoopla. Geniuses will always be better at juggling opposites, but now it's because of their thicker "corpus callosum," the fiber bridge that connects the two cerebral hemispheres (which is also denser in lefties and women). The left cortex handles details and logic, while the right processes wholes and intuition. Those with a denser fiber connection between the two have greater "cross-talk" between the two modes, enabling them to perceive the forest and the trees at the same time.

If they can field this dizzy contradiction, they may be geniuses; if not, they might get confused and stutter (in fact, more lefties do). This resembles Rothenberg's "Janusian thinking," which also involves polar opposites. It makes sense that geniuses would be able to juggle inherent contradictions that tend to befuddle everybody else.

Back in ancient Athens, Aristotle was describing the balancing act this way:

> The ideas and fancies would remain undeveloped if the melancholic were not then able to look at this with a critical eye—a sober eye—a cool eye. **As one hears of the creative process today, there are moments of inspiration and moments of rational analysis, editing, criticism. It is only the melancholic who will naturally have both.** (4, emphasis mine)

Moreover, Aristotle clearly specifies that this is "not owing to disease but from natural causes" (5), but his emphasis on health tends to disappear whenever he's quoted. He did not equate melancholia with depression—these words would not be synonymous for many centuries. As late as 1470, theology professor Bartholomaeus Anglicus was declaring that "some melancoli is kindly, and som [sic] unkindly" (6), and a century after that, people were still holding Aristotle's benign view:

> There are melancholike constitutions, which keep within the bounds and limits of health, which if we credit ancient writers, are very large and wide. (7)

It took Robert Burton's *The Anatomy of Melancholy* (1621) to forge a permanent link between melancholy and depression; this momentous work will be discussed in its historical context a bit further on. But speaking of timelines, some translations of Aristotle show him using the word "atrabilious" (Latin for "having black bile"), another term for "depressed" that did not actually exist until the 1650s.

Each time subsequent beliefs and word usage are pinned on early Greek philosophers, it provides additional "evidence" that they themselves equated greatness and depression, giving this notion historical weight. In any case, it should be remembered that Aristotle was primarily a philosopher, not a scientist—he also writes that covered hair is less likely to turn gray, and that females, who have fewer teeth than men, aren't fully human (8).

Virtually everything written on the mad genius begins with a mis-stating of Plato or Aristotle or both; sometimes their successor Seneca gets in there too, although he claims he's only copying Aristotle when he says, "There is no great genius without some touch of madness" (9).

But once again, this "madness" was coveted and divinely imposed rather than a sign of inherent pathology: it was a golden gift that fa-cilitated art, not some ongoing fragility that hobbled the artist. Plato's concept was also explicitly detached and temporary: "It does not belong to the person. It is itself. It comes, and it will go" (10).

Tweaking Greek philosophy is a popular method for linking cre-ativity and madness. Fans of the mad genius tend to ignore any doubt or contradiction whenever they trot out somebody in a toga to make their case. They also never mention Plato's clear distinction between creative focus and genuine derangement:

Like a bird he [the poet] looks upwards, and because he ignores what is down here, he is accused of behaving like a madman. (11)

Medical historian George Rosen agrees. "Divine madness by no means implied the occurrence of actual mental disease," he writes, noting that "when dealing with the ideas of the ancients . . . we must always keep in mind the psychological differences that separate us from them" (12).

One major difference is the belief that gods are actively involved in the daily lives of mortals; as familiar, intimate, and flawed as fam-ily, they're forever meddling in human affairs. Today, such sightings are relatively rare and may even be considered a hallucination—but then we live in a world where more people believe in alien visitation than in divine inspiration.

Another method among mythers is to simply pull confirmation out of the air. For example, it seems that the favorite saying "Whom the gods wish to destroy, they first make mad"—which emphasizes the dark and destructive nature of divine visitation—never even existed. In combing through the original texts, classical scholar Ruth Padel found nothing but suggestive fragments of this familiar phrase (13). Even *Bartlett's Familiar Quotations* relegates it to the throw-away category of "Latin saying—anonymous" (14). But it remains in circulation and surfaces now and again to "prove" that great creativity is a dangerous thing.

I do not believe scholars are deliberately withholding any of this information. It's more likely that they're not aware of it, since—according to the custom in creativity and madness research—they're just passing along the package they received, without questioning its origin or contents.

A Thousand Years of Darkness

THWACK! (THAT'S THE SOUND of the pendulum hitting the opposite wall.) After the fond Olympians left the stage, it didn't take long for the genius to turn from divine to witchy. The possibility was always there, since "the artist has always had the capacity to enchant and bewitch an audience" (15). But in this period, artists had to be careful not to shine their light too brightly, lest they be accused of heresy.

Not surprisingly, the devil entered the discussion with the ascendancy of the Catholic Church. The millennium between the fifth and fifteenth centuries was not a terribly good time for the exceptional mind, given all the attempts to link it to Satan. These years began with what Renaissance Italians later called the Dark Ages, in order to contrast their own enlightenment with their knuckle-dragging ancestors.

As always, social, political, economic, and local streams splashed together to create the current of the time. The fall of the Roman Empire had fragmented secular power so that public order was scattered in small feudal communities all over Europe. Lords, ladies, and their serfs retreated behind thick stone walls that were supposed to protect them from marauding barbarians and other thieves, but also "crammed the houses of the town together along crooked, filthy streets and exacerbated the burghers' proclivity to mass paranoia" (16). For societies in survival mode, suspicions and furies are easily kindled.

It also helps when they're formalized. Trying to keep control over its far-flung faithful, the Church relied on the heretic-hunting frenzy of the Inquisition, which introduced new tortures for unbelievers (and not coincidentally, confiscated their property). Born in France in 1184, it reached its familiar dramatic peak in Spain in the fourteenth and fifteenth centuries and actually remained on the books until 1834.

The Middle Ages, at least in Western culture, were a time of social upheaval, political disarray, and stalled intellectual progress. Poverty and disease were rampant, and most people did not live past their midthirties. The seven Crusades between 1095 and 1291 funneled people's frustrations into messianic zeal, promising earthly rewards and heavenly forgiveness to those who would join the war against the "infidels" who had "stolen" the Holy Land. Although many Crusaders were pious, there were also "people's crusades"—mobs fired up by local preachers that blindly headed for Jerusalem after murdering prosperous Jews in their own cities, and slaughtering other innocents along the way (17).

The fabled chaos and misery of this era was increased by a series of unfortunate natural events. It rained so steadily in the spring of 1315 that the food supply did not recover until 1325, causing widespread famine and millions of deaths. During this same century, a third of the European population was wiped out by the bubonic plague, or Black Death, a terror that lasted more than twenty years. Such an atmosphere provides little time or inclination for leisurely contemplation of Great Ideas; in this fragmented world, any pockets of enlightenment were surrounded by fog and out of touch with one another.

It was not until 1445, when the first book (the Gutenberg Bible) was published, that the Western world began blinking out of its long sleep of ignorance (18); then it would have tangible and durable means for the widespread sharing of ideas. But in the Middle Ages, intellectual activity was restricted to scattered monasteries, which were the sanctuaries for education and learning.

One influential thinker was Hildegard, the prominent German abbess, who taught that melancholy was a religious problem, caused by original sin. In 1151, she called it "the first attack by the devil on the nature of man since man disobeyed God's command by eating the apple." In classic "faces in a cloud" fashion, Hildegard's views may have been tinted by her own discomfort with carnality.

For instance, when describing the male melancholic, she says the "devil rages so powerfully in the passions of these men that they would kill the women with whom they are having sexual relations if they could." And women are "more healthy, more powerful, and happier without a mate than with one because they become sick from relations with a husband" (19). For Hildegard, melancholy was an unavoidable part of the human condition, but its specifics seemed to emerge from her own experience (or lack thereof?). In any case, this was not a hospitable time for genius—melancholic or otherwise.

From Sinners to Celebrities

WHEN FRAMED AS a religious problem, melancholy was much more ambiguous and flexible than it later became, initially covering everything from normal moods, sloth, character, and personality to mental disorders, ranging from mild to serious. It fell to Renaissance scholar Marsilio Ficino (1433–1499), a melancholic himself, to make it a symptom of genius.

Supported by banker Cosimo de' Medici, who financed his elaborate manuscripts, Ficino translated the works of Plato into Latin, producing his immensely popular *Three Books on Life*. He also founded the Florentine Academy, an informal school of writers and artists, whose purpose was to discuss these principles.

Ficino extolled the genius while keeping a wary eye on the Church, referring to "the high doors of the Muses" to which God, "who is omnipotent, [may] lead us and open them by miraculous power" (20). With a few simple tweaks, Plato's gift from the gods (small cap, plural) became the inspiration bestowed by God (The Only). With a few more, he closed the ancient circle by conflating Aristotle's melancholy with Plato's divine madness, and "the Renaissance accepted Ficino's conclusion: only the melancholic temperament was capable of Plato's creative enthusiasm" (21).

By his third volume, Ficino also managed to include astrology in order to further anoint himself as a genius. Now, in addition to being melancholic, one sure sign was being born under the sign of Saturn (as he was): "The highest of the planets embodies, and also bestowed, the highest and noblest faculties of the soul, reason, and speculation" (22).

And so the focused worship of genius really began in Renaissance Florence. But before strolling those sun-baked cobblestones, it's useful to note that Plato believed in divine inspiration only for poets. He thought painters and sculptors were simply imitating nature, not creating something inspired by the gods. Accordingly, "not until the Renaissance were visual artists credited with genuine ecstasy" (23). Not surprisingly, this was also when they first became stars.

At this point, the genius caught the great wave of enlightenment and discovery. The invention of the printing press, together with a new supply of cheap paper, made it easier to disseminate knowledge, including the wisdom of antiquity. The Florentine upswing even had financing, since three generations of wealthy Medicis were happy to patronize the arts; Lorenzo the Magnificent, himself a poet and musician, commissioned some of the greatest artists who ever lived. It's astonishing to realize that Leonardo, Rafael, Botticelli, Titian, and Michelangelo all walked this planet at the same time, and in the same forty square miles.

Of this group, Leonardo and Michelangelo have stimulated the most ink about genius. Michelangelo appears on psychologist Kay Jamison's widely cited list of 166 crazy dead creatives (featured in chapter 5), although she makes no attempt to explain his bipolar diagnosis (24). As Renaissance historian Paul Johnson reminds us,

> More nonsense has been written about [Michelangelo] than about any other great artist: that he was a neurotic, a homosexual, a

neo-Platonist mystic, etc. In fact he was nothing more than a very skilled and energetic artist, though often a very harassed one, who got himself into contractual messes, not always of his own devising. (25)

Although Leonardo da Vinci was admired in his lifetime as the sage, the magus, and the Man of Genius, according to Renaissance historian Richard Johnson, he was also "a distracted and ill-disciplined polymath" who was difficult to work with and employ:

> No one who saw anything done by him, even a mere drawing, failed to admire him, and he was in constant demand by the mightiest patrons . . . but his glittering career was punctuated by rows over intolerable delays, disputes over money, presumably arising from his unbusinesslike methods, and repetitive simple failures to do what he had promised. He was not in the least lazy, as some artists are, or tiresomely perfectionistic. But his final public output was meager. (26)

Incredibly, "there are only ten surviving paintings that are generally accepted as his." So was he a mad genius, or not?

Well, the genius part is obvious: Leonardo, interested in everything from weather to weaponry, inventor of the helicopter, is still considered the consummate Renaissance man because of his broad curiosity and capabilities: "He epitomized the questing spirit and the desire to excel in every possible way" (27). But his supposed madness is murky, especially from this great distance—it's entirely possible that Leonardo was only heedless or scattered or immature. And since he's not on the aforementioned famous list, he must simply be eccentric.

The Church took a dim view of all this genius worship. When Florence became leaderless after the death of Lorenzo the Magnificent, the French king invaded and put the Dominican monk Girolamo Savanarola in charge of a new republic. Savanarola had a long, irrational list of "moral laxities" to shout about, and his first official act was to make homosexuality punishable by death. His power peaked three years later, when he literally ignited the original bonfire of the vanities.

On February 7, 1497, whipped into paranoia by their frothing friar, Florentines raced to the public square to burn their most sinful items—among them, mirrors, cosmetics, chess pieces, and musical instruments. But the monk's objections to money finally alienated his followers, and exactly one year later, he was burned on the same spot. Fortunately, he could not prevent the Renaissance light from illuminating the rest of Europe. The artist was in full ascension.

At the same time, it was still prudent to tiptoe around the Church, which had recently begun using the *Malleus Maleficarum* (Witches' Hammer) to identify and punish witches. This 1485 manual was a great demented muddle of sin, sex, spells, and alleged mental disorders. Nor was this the end of the Church's mistrust of heretical thinkers—in 1616 Galileo was accused of claiming the earth revolved around the sun, rather than being the center of the universe, but he wasn't convicted and put under house arrest until 1636.

The Age of Fluid Retention

THWACK! Now THE PENDULUM swings again, and the focus shifts from imagination to intellect. This was the Age of Reason, which began somewhere in the early 1600s but ended precisely in 1789, with the start of the very unreasonable French Revolution. During this period—the flip side of the Renaissance—it now fell to the rational mind, rather than artistic vision, to interpret the world and humanity's place in it.

This new attitude was summarized by French philosopher Rene Descartes, who was looking for certainty outside the narrow teachings of the Church—a risky business, given it was just a year since Galileo was condemned for his blasphemous claims. But in 1637, Descartes went on record with his most famous saying: "cogito, ergo sum"—"I think, therefore I am." He made the content of a thought less important than the mind that produced it: whether the idea was false or true, the emphasis was on the "I" doing the thinking.

On the mechanical front, the 1712 debut of the steam engine led the way for a dazzling series of inventions that would forever transform manufacturing and transportation, as well as the pace and quality of life. Given society's growing faith in machines, it was natural to view the body as another one, and so humans became walking networks of tubes through which liquid energy circulated their impulses and emotions.

Just like the old Greek humors, these juices were essential to proper human functioning. Those who depleted them with foolish excesses were called "maniacs"—on autopsy, their brains were revealed to be unusually "hard, dry, and brittle" (28). Women were warned not to think too much, as this could compromise their fertility (29).

This strict focus on rationality made the emotional expansiveness of the Renaissance seem foolish and even dangerous. Now, ideas themselves could be physically threatening—particularly the more grandiose ones that a genius might express—since they might cause nervous exhaustion or "neurasthenia," the forerunner of today's equally murky Chronic Fatigue Syndrome. "From now on, one fell ill from too much feeling," says Michel Foucault in his fascinating history of the period. Ordinary habits could also lead to serious disease; a prominent fitness expert of the day listed such threats to health as

> novel reading, theater-going, immoderate thirst for knowledge, [and] too fierce a passion for sex or that other criminal habit, as morally reprehensible as it is physically harmful. (30)

Eventually, "that other criminal habit" (masturbation) was also said to cause epileptic seizures, which have been connected with madness as well (31). Worst of all, too much emotion—whether from passion, fear, shame, or joy—could even bring on sudden death (32).

During this period, the linkage of melancholy to depression was cemented by Robert Burton's influential *The Anatomy of Melancholy,* which, despite its title, was neither a medical reference nor confined to melancholy. It's actually a rambling, tumbling, and witty meditation on life—idleness, he says, is the "nurse of naughtiness"—combining his own speculations, Latin paraphrases, thousands of other people's opinions, and quotations from the Bible.

Anatomy addresses a wide range of human interests, including geography and goblins. First published in 1621, this popular 988-page tome was revised and reprinted at least five times during his life, with three more editions after his death (accounts vary). Despite the fact that no original manuscript has survived, a 1932 edition was reprinted in 2001.

Burton was a theologian and depressive who wrote to keep his own mind out of the muck. He claimed his insights were more accurate than those of other experts because "they get their knowledge by bookes, I mine by melancholising." Burton discusses the various types of melancholy and their causes, including demon possession and bad parenting: "If a man escapes a bad Nurse, he may be undone by evil bringing up" (33). He echoes Aristotle's concept of the benign melancholy that produces exceptional wit, as long as this humor is neither too hot nor too cold. He also provides a long list of cures to rectify "the passions and perturbations of the mind," with a section especially devoted to the healing powers of music.

Burton was likely inspired by the *Treatise of Melancholy* (1583), in which British doctor Philip Barrough offered some sensible cures that might be tried today, once its spellings were updated:

> Let the sicke ryde or walke by places pleasant and greene, or use sailing on water. Also a bath of sweet water with a moist dyet let the sicke use often as one of his remedies, sleep is wonderfull good for them, as also moderate carnall copulation. Let them be mery as much as may be, and heare musicall instruments and singing. (34)

On the other hand, forget it. No pharmaceuticals.

Barely Human

DURING THE AGE of Reason, people expected that human activity should be organized and predictable, like the rest of the natural world; when Newton explained gravity and motion, it suggested that behavioral laws could be discovered as well. By 1735, when Carl Linneaus classified all life forms by genus and species, he encouraged the idea that tidy sorting was the key to understanding the world. The words "tidy" and "genius" seem inherently incompatible, and in fact there was little room in this atmosphere for anyone who colored outside the lines.

Although official psychiatric labeling would not begin until 1853 with early notions of schizophrenia, rules about objectionable conduct were beginning to solidify in the public mind. Historian George Rosen describes it this way:

> Endowed with reason, man was expected to behave rationally, that is, according to accepted social standards . . . Eccentric or irrational behavior, actions which diverged from accepted norms, were considered as rooted in error or as derangement of the will, and therefore subject to correction. (35)

Confinement and restraint were used to "rehabilitate" the obstinate, who were considered barely human and a favorite source of entertainment. London's famous "Bedlam"—aka St. Mary's of Bethlehem Hospital—exhibited its lunatics to the public every Sunday. It's said that asylum windows were originally barred, not to keep lunatics from escaping, but to protect them from the curious and sadistic. In 1815 alone, there were 96,000 visits to Bedlam, according to a report to the House of Commons: "Visitors were charged a penny a visit, and for this they could tease the inmates to their heart's content," including poking them with long sticks (36).

This punitive approach to the mentally disordered gave them the same social taint as lepers, the last group that society had gathered up and penned in. As Foucault tells it,

> Every psychiatrist . . . yielded, at the beginning of the 19th cen-
> tury, to the same impulse of indignation; everywhere we find
> the same outrage, the same virtuous censure. No one blushed
> to put the insane in prison. (37)

It's no surprise that a machine-besotted society would find mechanical remedies for disordered behavior as well. One of the more
dramatic was the "rotatory machine," a chair or bed attached to a mov-
able bar, which was fastened to a stationary pillar. Patients were seated
and then spun at various speeds and intervals—a process known as
the "centrifugation of melancholy"—until their fluids were properly
blended (38). Incredibly, this method was used for nearly four decades,
from 1800 until 1836.

In 1818, physician W. S. O'Halloran introduced an improved
version that could spin four patients simultaneously, at one hundred
times a minute. This caused bleeding from the nose and ears and eventually, unconsciousness; whatever else it was supposed to accomplish,
it was certainly subduing. This smoothie technique was slightly more
merciful than the "bath of surprise," which involved a trapdoor and
unexpected immersion in ice water.

From Reason to Passion

IN THE EARLY 1800s, the flame of reason began to sputter in a fresh
and bracing wind of change. Order and regularity were surrendering
to exuberance and revelation; faith in science was being trumped by
trust in individual perception, and the focus on all those whiz-bang
inventions was replaced by worship of nature. Leading the parade of
Romantic poets to come, William Wordsworth cried, "My heart leaps
up when I behold a rainbow in the sky" (39). How very unscientistic
of him. THWACK!

In this new era, cold certainties dissolved into a hot brew of mystery
and passion. Who needs reason when "Beauty is truth, truth beauty /
that is all ye know on earth / And all ye need to know" (40)? In the

histrionic style of the age, John Keats began another poem with "I cry your mercy—pity—love!—aye, love!" (41). Humorist George Bernard Shaw, writing in his capacity as music critic, described how Beethoven thundered away from the prevailing classical style:

> It was this turbulence, this deliberate disorder, this mockery, this reckless and triumphant disregard of conventional manners, that set Beethoven apart from the musical geniuses of the ceremonious seventeenth and eighteenth centuries. He was a giant wave in [the] storm of the human spirit which produced the French Revolution. (42)

Frankenstein was born in 1818, adding to the delectable shivering from Gothic horror tales and revelations from the spirit world. Mediums proliferated, including the notorious Madame Helena Blavatsky. She founded the popular Theosophical Society, the beginning of New Age thinking, which still exists today (43).

Romantic poets dramatized their "otherness" and—buckle up, here we go—enthusiastically encouraged the idea that the most noble art comes from the greatest torment. Percy Bysshe Shelley—a free-love advocate who was kicked out of Oxford for atheism—explicitly referred to his poetry as "harmonious madness" (44). In discussing John Milton, the critic Lord Macaulay writes, "Perhaps no person can be a poet, or even enjoy poetry, without a certain unsoundness of mind" (45). (This brings up a question that tugs at the sleeve of this whole enterprise: if artists must be thoroughly unhinged in order to produce their greatest work, how can a relatively hinged audience ever properly appreciate what they create?)

Across the pond in Baltimore, the alcoholic Edgar Alan Poe was also pondering the connection between creativity and madness, with words that have acquired a clinical weight:

> The question is not yet settled, whether madness is or is not the loftiest intelligence—whether much that is glorious—whether

all that is profound—does not spring from disease of thought—
from moods of mind exalted at the expense of the general intellect. (46)

The Romantic era launched the heroic figure that became the quint-
essential mad genius: inspired, moody, tortured. The artists had their
own hands in this development, making it fashionable to be dreamy
and sad. In his *Madness: A Brief History* (2002), social historian Roy
Porter writes, "While permitting displays of superfine sensibilities,
these complaints served as signs of social superiority, for the ailments
were exclusive to truly refined temperaments" (47).

In many ways the Romantic poets were the rock stars of their day,
complete with extravagant behavior and tragic deaths. In 1821, Keats died of TB at the age of twenty-five. A year later, Shelley, barely
thirty, drowned in Italy, where he'd gone to live because of scandal,
including the suicides of two women he was courting (48). Less than
two years after that, thirty-six-year-old Byron succumbed to a fever
in Messolonghi, where he was either heroically fighting for Greek independence or hiding out to escape debts and rumors at home. Such
endings strengthen their artistic legacies, as well as every armchair
diagnosis of their madness.

All told, the Romantic era was the peak historical period for mad
genius, setting the conventions for attitudes and behaviors that still
define them today.

FOUR

The Rise of Righteous Rumor

Inspect every piece of pseudoscience and you will find a
security blanket, a thumb to suck, a skirt to hold. What
does the scientist have to offer in exchange? Uncertainty!
Insecurity!

~ *Isaac Asimov*

THE ROMANTIC ERA FOCUS ON passion, rule breakers, and the
occult was a natural THWACK to the previous glorification of
reason. Not surprisingly, following the swinging pendulum's inevitable
path, all this extravagance created its own backlash.

In the late nineteenth century, when science hoisted itself to the
top of society's pedestal, it not only pushed the geniuses off, but made
sure they would never get that high again. Sociologist-historian George
Becker puts it this way:

> This essentially Romantic image of the extraordinary man as one
> who creates his works from instinctive necessity was to become,
> quite ironically, a primary basis for the "scientific" or "clinical"
> claims on behalf of the genius-madness association. (1)

Whenever society recoils from excess, it opens the door for the
methodical approach to rush in. And this time it came roaring back
with a vengeance, trumpeting some brand-new dogma about creative

weakness in which the exceptional mind, already riddled with madness, was doomed to inherited degeneracy as well. THA-WACK!

Degenerates and Lunatics

IN THE MID-1800s, physicians who performed sanity evaluations for the courts were known as "alienists." This term reflected the perception (and fervent hope) that the mentally disordered were far removed from so-called normal people. The new science of heredity fed this view by making them qualitatively different, suffering from inherent biological flaws that other people did not possess.

This affected attitudes toward treatment, since if madness comes from inherited weakness rather than willful misbehavior, society can pity its deviants rather than punish them. (Arguably, not much of an improvement.) Although they were still locking them up, there was a budding interest in understanding and perhaps even curing them.

As usual, this attitude change was a product of intersecting currents in the larger society. The Industrial Revolution had greatly expanded the number of menial urban jobs and vagrants seeking them; as a result, the slums were sprawling and the underclass was growing, especially in London. The official 1844 Lunacy Report called for more licensed facilities to handle the disturbed, which by now included the smelly and staggering and those who couldn't pay their debts. In fact, "pauper lunatics" made up the great majority of committals, with "habitual intemperance" listed as their primary cause of insanity. Translation: they were broke and drunk.

Such undesirables, formerly housed in prisons and the basements of public buildings, were now kept in asylums, where petty criminals, drifters, epileptics, "idiots," and the variously "incurable" all crowded together. People exhibiting the bizarre behaviors of tertiary syphilis were sent there too, because there was little understanding of this disease and no test for it until 1906 (its link to madness is explained in chapter 6).

In exploring the lineage of insanity, researchers now had a large, captive population to work with; they could easily question confined inmates about their family histories. Those whose lives were less stable, happy, and productive than their parents' provided "proof" that their ailments were degenerative, especially when environmental stressors like poverty and overcrowding were left out of the equation (2).

Soon genius became a degenerative condition as well. The idea was formally introduced by French psychiatrist Benedict-Augustin Morel in his two-volume groundbreaking text on "maladies mentales" (1852–53). It was advanced by his colleague Jacques-Joseph Moreau de Tours, who published seven hundred pages on the "traits of degeneration" that carried genius and lunacy together through the ages. According to Moreau, geniuses suffer from "a morbid nervous affliction" that compels them to follow their "bursts of imagination" at the expense of their will and reason (3). He explains that "originality of thought and quickness and preponderance of the intellectual faculties [are] organically much the same thing as madness and idiocy" (4).

By this time, those old, exultant notions of divine inspiration and Romantic creation were in full retreat, fleeing the dangerous genius and his appalling infirmities. Now there was "a most curious, sad, and perverse linking together of genius and mental disorder" (5). These early inheritance theories linger in today's mythology, fueling the continuing guesswork about genetics.

As always, politics played its part—particularly the notion that it was England's duty to absorb and enlighten "barbaric" places like India and Egypt (two of the world's oldest civilizations, where they were refining their literature and art while the Celts were still worshipping rock circles). As the British Empire expanded, it intensified the Victorian fear of being overrun by those swarthy, ill-mannered "others."

This haughty attitude found its ultimate voice in Rudyard Kipling's popular poem "The White Man's Burden" (1899), which coined that loathsome phrase while describing "Your new-caught sullen peoples / Half devil and half child." "Half devil and half child" fit quite neatly into the new opinion of genius. In any case, this was the ideal climate for affirming the superiority of the "betters" by documenting the unavoidable taint of the "lessers"—whether they were criminals, lunatics, primitives, or those degenerate geniuses. It was a natural, if twisted, outgrowth of evolution.

That new science had emerged in 1859, when Charles Darwin launched the idea of inborn advantage in his *Origin of the Species*. Seven years later, Gregor Mendel described how the inheritance mechanism works. But it was Darwin's cousin Francis Galton who pushed the explicit link between exceptional minds and insanity.

Probably a genius himself, Galton invented statistical correlation, the weather map, fingerprinting, and the dog whistle. He also had at least one severe nervous breakdown, which could easily account for his passionate belief that high ability and madness are "painfully close" (faces in a cloud, again). In his masterpiece *Hereditary Genius*, Galton offers a theory that is still in circulation today:

> Those who are over-eager and extremely active in mind must often possess brains that are more excitable and peculiar than is consistent with soundness. They are likely to become crazy at times, and perhaps to break down altogether. (6)

The Pale, Stammering Genius

IN ONE OF history's perfect storms, it happens that all these budding ideas about creative pathology were sprouting just as psychiatrists were asserting their legitimacy:

> In the late nineteenth century the priority lay, for many psychiatrists, upon establishing their discipline as a truly scientific enterprise, capable of taking its rightful place in the pantheon of the "hard" biomedical sciences, along with neurology and pathology, and utterly distinct from such quackish and fringy embarrassments as mesmerism and spiritualism. (7)

This might account for some of the ferocious certainty that came next.

Today Morel and Moreau de Tours are mere footnotes to the Italian "professor of legal medicine" Cesare Lombroso, the father of the psychological autopsy and the notion of the "born criminal." Lombroso attacked the exceptional person like an all-you-can-eat buffet—poring over biographical dictionaries, encyclopedias, autobiographies, letters, and assorted creative products, he hunted the essence of the eminent, whom he variously referred to as abnormal, morbid, insane, gifted, and genius.

Lombroso also scrutinized their facial symmetry and skull size for anomalies he called "stigmata," a deliberate religious reference that conveyed the reverent awe geniuses frequently inspire—as well as the doom that surely awaits them. In his view, they were certainly riddled with physical defects.

For instance, in *The Man of Genius* (1891), Lombroso announces that people of high ability are usually small, pasty, and emaciated. Prone to rickets, amnesia, prominent ears, "excessive originality," and "inadequate beard," they also tend to be sexually sterile, left-handed, and stammering "restless vagabonds." But this was to be expected:

> Just as giants pay a heavy ransom for their stature in sterility and relative muscular and mental weakness, so the giants of thought expiate their intellectual force in degeneration and psychoses. It is thus that the signs of degeneration are found more frequently in men of genius than even in the insane. (8)

Although Lombroso's peers called his scholarship "shoddy" and his "colossal mass of anecdotal data" only "superficially persuasive," the same shotgun approach has been used by researchers ever since (9).

Today's mad genius advocates tend to reference Lombroso's work, but not its embarrassing details. For instance, Andreasen only mentions that Lombroso "argued for the hereditary nature of creativity and madness" (10), while Jamison just identifies him as someone who "wrote extensively about the relationship between mental illness and genius" (11). Neither mentions those skinny, stammering, flop-eared vagabonds who struggle to produce facial hair. Nor does anyone else who climbs up on his reputation to make their case.

But Lombroso's silliness was not unique. In his day, many believed in phrenology, the "science" of connecting skull features to personality types. This led to pronouncements about the heads of "reasoning maniacs" that contained "an antero-posterior curve less than that of sane persons, lunatics and imbeciles, and even of idiots" (12). This idea was later expanded by Kretschmer to link body shape to mental "illness"; as late as 1993, writer Honore de Balzac was diagnosed as manic-depressive because he had the short legs and big belly of the "pyknic" type (13).

By now, the idea of the lopsided, stunted, or otherwise damaged creative was so popular that J. F. Nisbet's *The Insanity of Genius* enjoyed six printings after its debut in 1891. Since then, his words have been carefully edited to fit the mad genius agenda. For example, there's no sign of the nuance he introduced: the gradations of "mental unsoundness" that create "imperfect" or "fractional" geniuses; nor does anyone repeat his warning that "no trustworthy percentages can be arrived at" (14).

Like Lombroso, Nisbet is only credited for providing "suggestive clues to the significantly increased rates of mood disorders and suicide in eminent writers and artists" (15), although these early scientists did more than that:

> They had shifted the inquiry into art and artists from philosophical speculations to medical research and, though misapprehending the Aristotelian concept of the "mad" and "melancholic" genius, had given the old tradition of the link between genius and abnormal psychological conditions a pseudoscientific basis. (16)

This was used to explain some of the great artists of the time, including composer Frederic Chopin, whose biographer confidently diagnosed him with "hyperaesthesia" [hypersensitivity], "the penalty of **all** sick genius." He also suffered from paralyzing stage fright, according to his contemporary Franz Liszt, who quoted Chopin's complaint of feeling "suffocated by the panting breath of the public" (17). Much like today's audience, the public of a century ago was eager to learn what was wrong with their creative icons.

They got an extensive list from physician Theophilius Bulkeley Hyslop, one of Virginia Woolf's four doctors, with a name that could not be invented. In *The Great Abnormals* (1925), Hyslop devotes a full fifty-eight pages to "the peculiarities of the men of genius," including the news that Mozart's opera *Don Giovanni* was inspired by the sight of an orange. Hyslop also found it "peculiar" that John Milton needed to hear music before beginning to write, and that Haydn claimed he could attain inspiration by praying for it (18).

Hyslop also worried that since "degenerates often turn their unhealthy impulses toward art," they might attain a large following and thereby pervert the standards of taste (19). If this sounds more like a protective critic than a physician, it's because Hyslop was himself an accomplished painter, composer, and musician. As such, even when he claims that "it must be conceded, by even the intolerant of degeneration-mongering, that genius is indeed akin to madness," he is more sympathetic than most. Moreover, he was one of the first to acknowledge the social stress that geniuses encounter:

> If he be eccentric, unconventional, or abnormal in his behavior, he is treated with ridicule by the community, irrespective of the fact that he may be a God-fearing, law-abiding, self-supporting, and responsible human being . . . **Many of the world's geniuses have had to seek asylum or protection against the intolerance displayed by their fellow beings**. (20, emphasis mine)

Finally, it's impossible to discuss creative vulnerability without a salute to Freud, for whom life was full of suffering; we've also reached his chronological niche. The growth of Freud's influence and the recruitment of his disciples began with *Interpretation of Dreams* (1900) and especially *The Psychopathology of Everyday Life* (1901), which introduced the idea of the "Freudian slip" (a handy concept, whatever you may think of the rest of his theories).

Freud's power and fan base spread steadily for another thirty years, and despite decades of Freud-bashing, his belief in our eternal struggles—and his dread of what slithers beneath them—continue to intrigue and inspire. Freud's involuntary creative feeds right into the mad genius idea—after all, the trance of helpless possession will always be fascinating, whether the victim swoons with id or inspiration.

So does his fear of intense emotion. In his classic triple-tier model of the mind, the civilized functions of conscience (superego) and reason (ego) can barely contain the primitive, selfish, shrieking id that lives downstairs. Creatives are at special risk, because they spend so much time in the id's territory. Here's how I explained it in 2002:

> Unreliably contained by reason, [these strong and primitive emotions] threaten our stability during the day and sneak out at night to do their mischief in dreams. The artist who deliberately explores this realm for his raw material is therefore in greater danger of losing control: he spends his life walking around the rim of a volcano. (21)

People have long speculated about the nature of Freud's relentless pessimism. I recently stumbled on a clue: he disliked music, seeing it as "solely an intrusion." According to his nephew Harry, among others, music was his least favorite of the arts; as a child, he objected so strongly to his sister's piano lessons that his parents had the offending instrument removed (22).

Given his constricted perspective, we can easily understand why Freud would have avoided anything that could whip up powerful and unexpected feelings. But his musical aversion also deprived him of its unique nourishment and balm. Certainly, his sour and mechanistic worldview, however fascinating, offers very little comfort to anyone.

Although Shakespeare predated Freud by several centuries, I think the Englishman nailed the Viennese when he wrote,

The man that hath no music in himself,
Nor is not moved with concord of sweet sounds,
Is fit for treasons, stratagems and spoils;
The motions of his spirit are dull as night,
And his affections dark as Erebus;
Let no such man be trusted. Mark the music. (23)

Voices of Dissent

IT'S ALWAYS EASIER to connect creativity and madness when dissenting opinions are overlooked. In a sea of Galtons, Lombrosos, and Nisbets, few quote the influential psychiatrist Jean-Etienne Dominque Esquirol, author of the first psychiatric textbook (1845), who wrote,

> Men of the greatest geniuses, both in the sciences and the arts, the most illustrious poets, the most skillful painters, have preserved their reason, even to extreme old age. (24)

William James, the first great American psychologist, is also conspicuously absent from these discussions; it might be his sympathetic attitude toward altered states, which he felt were unjustly degraded by those who hadn't experienced them:

> One must have musical ears to know the value of a symphony; one must have been in love oneself to understand a lover's state of mind. Lacking the heart or ear, we cannot interpret the musician or the lover justly, and are even likely to consider him weak-minded or absurd.

James rings the big bell with this observation. Going on to address Messrs. Moreau, Lombroso, and Nisbet by name, he brings up another central concern of his (and mine) when he asks,

Now do these authors, after having succeeded in establishing to their own satisfaction that the works of genius are fruits of disease, consistently proceed thereupon to impugn the value of the fruits? . . . Do they frankly forbid us to admire the productions of genius from now onwards? (25)

Then there's physician Havelock Ellis, who declares quite clearly in his *Study of British Genius* that "we must put out of court any theory as to genius being a form of insanity" (26). In fact, after his 1927 examination of one thousand British geniuses, Ellis actually "rejected all views of genius and insanity as concomitant," noting a host of environmental factors that could affect the mental health of creative people, such as "impoverishment, rejection [and] persecution" (27).

But his credibility was apparently compromised by his association with sexual deviations: he wrote about homosexuality and transgenderism and was known to have married a lesbian. (Another "faces in a cloud" moment—Ellis spent most of his career studying sex without being able to perform it; perhaps he was looking for the key, since he was reportedly impotent until the age of sixty.)

In *The Problem of Genius* (1932), psychiatrist Wilhelm Lange-Eichbaum also argues for the broader social view, but few quote his inconvenient assertion that "one cannot be born a genius [since] they are created by mankind"—or his incisive observation: "The show that the public enjoys is more a creation of the audience than the actors" (28).

Being a sculptor and playwright probably gave him more tolerance than his colleagues were showing, as well as a keener awareness of the tough road ahead:

To become a man of genius means to be subjected, in the majority of cases and in accordance with theoretical principles, to a life of intense and gruesome martyrdom. (29)

The martyrdom may still be intense, but at least he acknowledges the outside pressures that burden and distract geniuses as they try to be true to their calling. In 1995, Eysenck echoed Lange-Eichbaum's belief (and the point of these last two chapters) that the view of genius changes as society does (30).

Stubborn Stigma

IN 1949 PSYCHIATRIST Adele Juda's research was posthumously published. After her carefully conducted scientific study of 294 geniuses and their families, Juda came to the opposite conclusion from Lombroso and his colleagues:

> There is no definitive relationship between highest mental capacity and psychic health or illness, and no evidence to support the assumption that the genesis of highest intellectual ability depends on psychic abnormalities. **The high number of mentally healthy geniuses speaks against such a claim and repudiates the slogan "genius and insanity."** (31, delighted emphasis mine)

As definitive as her conclusion was, it tends to get lost in the mad genius undertow. "Mentally healthy" will never be as interesting as "driven" and "doomed."

This was also the time frame in which it first became fashionable to contemplate one's own psychology (also known as "navel-gazing"). By the 1950s, it was widely accepted that mental disorder was not just for the certifiable—ordinary people might also have "neuroses" and "complexes." In 1956 psychiatrist Karl Menninger, a founder of the leading psychiatric clinic that still bears his name, claimed,

> Gone forever is the notion that the mentally ill person is an exception. It is now accepted that most people have some degree of mental illness at some time. (32)

This is always good news for the people and places that treat such things. At the time, Menninger's certainty dovetailed nicely with the rise of psychoanalysis as a status symbol, as many creatives—such as actors and writers connected with the Actor's Studio—believed that taking that perilous inner journey would add depth to their art. Woody Allen used to joke that he spent more years in analysis than out of it. And once upon a time, such long-term talk therapy was even covered by insurance; today, the only conversation that gets reimbursed is "how many refills do you need?"

It's easy to dismiss early notions of devil possession and "cretin-like physiognomy" as coming from a more ignorant time. But we haven't made that much progress—we've only invented more sophisticated ways to distance and demean our geniuses, and built an elaborate new scaffolding of pseudoscience to bolster the ancient myth. The irony is that despite society's normalization of psychopathology and the widespread use of its vocabulary, there's a lingering stigma toward the more serious disorders, and with it a continued suspicion of the mysterious power behind the genius.

This public mind-set complicates the professional lobbying for reimbursement parity, where psychological ailments are compared to physical illnesses like diabetes—a random neurochemical glitch that has no impact on a person's value. There's still a dark suspicion of the graver conditions, fears that create discrimination in housing and employment as well as restrictions on the right to vote, drive, and win custody of a child:

> These kinds of discrimination are often triggered simply by a history of mental disorder rather than by any documented disability. Media stereotypes . . . treat the entire topic with misinformation and even ridicule. (33)

A survey of over two thousand British and American citizens revealed considerable fear and revulsion in this area, concluding that "stigmas about mental illness seem to be widely endorsed by the general public." Moreover, these respondents tended to file mental disorder together with prostitution and criminality, suggesting that the creaky old theories of degeneration are still in play.

As a psychologist, I'm especially dismayed by the five studies showing that "even well-trained professionals from most mental health disciplines subscribe to stereotypes about mental illness" (34). It's sad when those who should be most sensitive to the damage of stigma are helping to perpetuate it—and this includes civilian advocates as well. In his superb book about his schizophrenic brother, Jay Neugeboren writes,

> Even at meetings and fund-raising dinners sponsored by chapters of the Alliance for the Mentally Ill or the Mental Health Association, most people who come up to me after I give a talk will wait until we are alone before they will confide, softly and hesitantly, and looking around first to make sure nobody can overhear, that they too have a brother or sister, son or daughter who suffers from mental illness. (35)

If these public champions feel shame in revealing their own connections, what hope is there for tolerance in society at large?

Where Are We Now?

THE NEXT GREAT flurry of questionable research began in the late 1970s, and will be dismantled in the next chapter. But since all good lessons end with a summary, here we go: despite centuries of attention, the concepts of creativity and madness are still as murky as ever. The only certainty lies in the millions of minds that believe they are connected.

These are not particularly good times for genius, except for Bill Gates, Steve Jobs, Mark Zuckerberg and all those other whiz kids who made their fortunes in technology. Artistic geniuses are still in the shadows—not just because pathology is in fashion, but because recent attitudes toward achievement have kept them there.

As I write this, the United States still ranks self-esteem higher than ability or effort. If students aren't succeeding and (gasp) might feel bad about themselves, we simply lower the passing grade—that is, assuming we're grading them at all. This protects them from the unthinkable blow of failure, which must be avoided despite any valuable life lessons that may come from it. Such practices help maintain the politically correct illusion that no one is inherently more capable than anyone else. Even the top achievers need coddling, as evidenced by the number of high schools that had multiple valedictorians in 2010 (Stratford High School in Houston, Texas, had thirty).

This insistence on level playing fields is reinforced by commercial messages that everyone "deserves" the house or the body or the job they desire, simply by wanting them (in what other climate could something like *The Secret* flourish?) All this entitlement can only breed resentment of exceptional talent.

So does the educational focus on rote testing at the expense of critical thinking—it creates minds that cannot make logical connections for themselves, thus becoming easy prey for the most compelling Internet rumor and seductive mythology, including the newest "findings" about the mad genius.

This disastrous testing policy, which should have been called "No Child Left Inspired," is one of the most dismaying legacies of Bush II, who also proved that mediocrity is no barrier to even the highest success. But no worries: if the expectation of reward without effort creates any chafing resentment toward geniuses and their unfair advantages, it can easily be soothed by focusing on their miserable lives.

And so the myth continues to denigrate the creatives and their products—and with a scientific legitimacy that is no better than Lombroso's. It's time to see what the research is made of.

PART THREE

Building on Sand

Premature Victories

Thus science must begin with myths, and with the criticism
of myths, neither with the collection of observations, nor
with the invention of experiments, but with critical discussion of myths and of magical techniques and practices.
~ *Karl Popper*, Conjectures and Refutations

N OW THE SEARCHLIGHT FALLS ON the most widely cited "proof"
of the mad genius myth, exposing the frayed edges and whis-
tling holes that are so often overlooked. Just in case I'd overstated the
problem, I hauled out my old statistics textbooks to check, and there
it was: the need for consensual clarity in the definition and measurement of variables, the importance of randomized and sufficient samples,
the advisability of replication, and the forthright acknowledgment of
extraneous factors that could muddy up the outcome.

You don't need a textbook to know that it's not kosher to begin
a study knowing what you hope to get, and then tweaking things to
make it happen. And the mad genius will never be legitimized by researcher motivation, no matter how passionate; or a theoretical hunch,
no matter how compelling; or even an intuitive list of great talents
who get their bipolar badges long after death.

But passion and hunches and postmortem lists are what the world
has settled for, since there's no scientific evidence that creatives suffer any
more than other occupational groups, and little interest in finding any.

As noted in chapter 1, it's not a priority for the NIMH or DRADA. Whenever they post their statistics—DRADA says about 14 percent of American adults suffer mood disorders each year, while NIMH and others report 9.5 percent (1)—no one knows the relative contribution of different occupational groups to that total.

This is because nobody asks. So far, DRADA's most extensive membership survey (1993) ignored occupation altogether, only asking if people had been fired or arrested, or had their educations interrupted because of their mood disorders. More recently (2005), NAMI did an online study of 1,086 self-described depressives, but since they partnered with Wyeth Pharmaceuticals, the focus was on medication, not job description; in any case, the idea of "self-described" depressives raises alarms all by itself.

On the rare occasions when studies do specify jobs, they tend to evaluate them by prestige rather than type, or use vague groupings like "minor professionals" that may or may not include any artists (2). In 2007, a huge online study in Australia looked at 17,000 people with depression, but these were all business professionals (the most depressed group turned out to be lawyers, followed by patent attorneys, for whatever that's worth).

In Pittsburgh, an ongoing bipolar genetic research project has only one question about work: "What is the most responsible job you ever had?"—an issue with little relevance to a freelance career. This comes from the standardized *Diagnostic Manual for Genetic Studies*, which also codes an occupational category for "writers, artists, entertainers and athletes" that rather muddies up the creative identity, a common practice, as we shall see (3).

Lost Chances

THE NIMH HAD a beautiful opportunity to clear some of this up for good, but they blew it. In 1999 they launched their STEP-BD study (Systematic Treatment Enhancement Program for Bipolar Disorder), a $22 million, eight-year search for the most effective treatments for bipolar disorder. With seventeen research sites and a final total of 4,361 participants, it was the largest such effort ever made in the United States. As such, it might have provided some answers to the age-old questions about the mad genius, except for one thing: nobody cared to ask.

In other words, there was no attempt to compare the frequency of bipolar disorder among creative people as opposed to any other occupational group. Although the six-page demographic form was exhaustively detailed—inquiring about type of residence and roommates, and whether people left work early or got there late—it provided no way for participants to identify themselves as committed creative freelancers. There was no place to check (or write in) musician or writer, painter or playwright, or anything else. The closest category was "craftsmen and kindred workers," which included "baker."

Clearly tailored for more conventional jobs, the form made sharp distinctions between "work" (paid) and "non-work" (unpaid) that freelancers cannot draw, given all the private, undocumented time they spend practicing and perfecting their skills and ideas. However essential such activities are to an artistic career, to STEP-BD—and to many relatives—they don't qualify as "work." And there was no room to explain that the end of a two-week music gig is not a "layoff" in the usual sense.

So I called Dr. Gary Sachs at Massachusetts General Hospital, one of STEP-BD's two principal investigators, and asked him if they had deliberately chosen to avoid the mad genius issue. "It didn't come up at all," he said, explaining that the study focused on public health and "was not set up to look at such lofty things." And while they made no "conscious decision" to exclude creative endeavors from the job categories, neither did they have "a burning desire" to include them (4).

This made perfect sense, since STEP-BD was designed to evaluate treatments for bipolar disorder, not who's more likely to get it. But a few questions about creative activity and identity, answered by thousands of bipolars who were study-verified—not just self-described—could have been helpful. (Whether or not you believe bipolar disorder is a legitimate entity, society treats it as if it is.) With its unprecedented size and reach, STEP might have produced powerful statistics about which groups are more vulnerable than others; perhaps it would have resolved the controversy, once and for all.

But it didn't. Instead, we still have countless inferences and unwarranted declarations, with some empirical sleight of hand thrown in for good measure, while the belief that creatives are more disturbed than everyone else continues to persist.

This is largely due to the work of just three people: psychiatrists Nancy Andreasen and Arnold Ludwig and especially psychologist Kay Jamison, whose prolific writings and public appearances have made her the mad genius go-to person for decades. The trio's influence is strengthened by every psychology textbook that mentions their work without comment, or any suggestion that other explanations are possible. This makes the mad genius seem like a done deal when it's anything but (I still think "hogwash" is a good descriptor) (5). Worst of all, this encourages future clinicians to use such stereotypes in their work with creative people.

Andreasen: The Groundbreaker

THE SO-CALLED LANDMARK study was conducted by psychiatrist Nancy Andreasen at the Iowa Writers' Workshop. Her interest in writers was longstanding: a PhD in Renaissance literature from the University of Nebraska, and then an English instructor at the University of Iowa, she switched to medicine after surviving a life-threatening postpartum infection.

Andreasen's stunning conclusion—that fully 80 percent of writers had mood disorders, compared with only 30 percent of non-writers—became the first brick in the new empirical foundation. Virtually all subsequent studies cite this one as critical experimental support despite the fact that in the fifteen years it took to complete—from its 1972 inception to its 1987 publication—Andreasen interviewed only thirty writers, all of whom she knew personally. This automatically compromises the value of her findings.

In fact, the study's design had enough weaknesses to sink that ship long before it sailed. These are revealed, along with problems in the work of Jamison and Ludwig, in my "Creative Mythconceptions: A Closer Look at the Evidence for the 'Mad Genius' Hypothesis," a detailed analysis published in a peer-reviewed journal of the American Psychological Association (6).

There is no need to translate all those arguments here, but it's crucial to include the study's biggest shortcomings, starting with that all-white, middle-aged, and male sample. Using such a specialized group automatically prevents Andreasen's findings from describing anyone outside the narrow confines of her sample, such as creative twenty-somethings, nonwhites, and women. Knowing your subjects personally is an additional drawback, especially when you are their sole examiner and judge.

It's also problematic that nobody questions the validity of Andreasen's supposedly "non-creative" comparison group. Perhaps some of these people do have artistic interests and even talents of their own—weekend watercolorists, say, or shower singers—even if they choose not to make a career of them. Doesn't that muddy her comparison to professional writers? And how did Andreasen determine that the control group's occupations (lawyer, social worker) "did not require high levels of creativity"? (7). Many lawyers and social workers might disagree.

Another snag involves definition and measurement. In order to produce that impressive 80 percent figure with only thirty people, Andreasen had to bundle together those who had serious problems with others who had a mild hypomanic experience "some time in their lives." The possibility that this could be the "high" of falling in love is not considered. In any case, the outcome depends on what people say about themselves, a method with questionable reliability (as the next chapter will show). All told, this is hardly the same thing as "proving" that "all" writers are seriously disturbed, which is how this study gets passed along from year to year, book to book, and mind to mind.

But dubious science never derails this train, and so the "news" that 80 percent of writers are mentally "ill" quickly spread to the world at large. It got a prepublication boost from *Psychology Today*, which in 1984 trumpeted "*the* striking association between creativity and manic depression," as if the study were not confined to writers (8). *Science News* quickly picked up the torch, claiming that this alleged broad-based association was "close" (9).

The irony is that Andreasen herself has admitted, both in print and in person, that her most-celebrated results are not "statistically significant"—that is, that she cannot rule out the impact of chance. But she trumps all criticism when she notes that two of those thirty writers eventually committed suicide. Any methodological weaknesses, she says, "pale before the clinical implications of this fact" (10).

Of course suicide is the ultimate clinical concern. But consider this: is it more humane to *assume* the special pathology of artists—expecting them to be damaged human beings—or to actually *prove* that this special pathology exists?

Either way, Andreasen soon left this murky arena altogether, earning great admiration and prestigious awards for her work on brain imaging and schizophrenia. It's likely that her subsequent status adds credibility to this early study, despite its essential flaws.

Jamison: Romanticizing Bipolar Disorder

ANDREASEN PROVIDED THE springboard for Kay Jamison, who has been called "the de facto point person for the art and madness link" (11). Certainly she's been its most persistent champion, which necessitates a little reality-tweaking here and there. For instance, in her most widely cited study (1989), Jamison claims that Andreasen's study showed "an exceptionally high rate of affective illness, especially bipolar" (12) as if there were no reason to question it.

Jamison may be silent because her work has similar flaws, creating a classic pot-and-kettle dilemma (13). Her method was to interview forty-seven award-winning British creatives—poets, playwrights, novelists, biographers, and visual artists—whom she (alone) questioned about their mood states and psychiatric histories. Like Andreasen's participants, they were all male and white, and mostly middle-aged, which once again precludes the fair application of results outside that gender, race, and age group, as well as to non–award winners.

But Jamison's conclusions, like Andreasen's, were impressive: 38 percent had sought treatment for depression or bipolar disorder, a rate she estimates as thirty times greater than that of the general population—and has been repeated without question ever since.

Equally startling is her 50 percent figure for poets, unless you happen to know that it represents only *nine* people; then there's her 12.5 percent figure for visual artists on antidepressants, which represents only *one* person. Yet whenever the study is mentioned, such details vanish and only the impressive percentages remain.

Hobbled by such limitations, this research can prove nothing at all. But you'd never know that without reading the original, given all the buzz about this "empirical confirmation" of creative madness. It helps that the original study is very hard to find, since it appeared in an obscure interdisciplinary newsletter published by the little-known Washington School of Psychiatry in Washington, DC. Given the publication's mainstream title of "Psychiatry," it's easy to assume that Jamison's work was published in a widely circulated, peer-reviewed journal, which lends more credence to her results than their true setting would permit.

My guess is that most professionals haven't seen it, and simply pass the dramatic conclusions along from other researchers who haven't read it either—everyone believing that someone along the chain has done the proper vetting. In fact, both this study and Andreasen's are disseminated as if they really do demonstrate "very high rates of psychopathology" among creative people. They are commended as "controlled statistical studies" with "overwhelmingly consistent" results, part of "a substantial body of literature that describes significant statistical relationships between bipolar disorder and creativity" (14).

Back to basics: by definition, it's impossible to have a controlled study without a control *group*, and you cannot evaluate differences *between* groups if you only have one group to work with. That's why Jamison only reports simple percentages: her lack of a comparison sample made it impossible for her to use real statistics. But she still refers to her study as "rigorous" support for her claim that "a high number of established artists—far more than could be expected by chance—meet the diagnostic criteria for manic depression or major depression" (15).

This last statement is also misleading, since referring to "the" diagnostic criteria implies that standardized guidelines were followed when they were not. Instead, Jamison's study rides on the unique assumption that seeking treatment for something is the same thing as having it. As she explains, "Specific diagnostic criteria were not used in this study as the primary aim was to ascertain actual rates of treatment, a more stringent criterion for severity of affective illness" (16). This is a minority opinion, at best.

Jamison has criticized psychiatry's definitions as "staggeringly desiccated" and unable to capture the true essence of madness (17). This may be true, but it doesn't mean you can invent your own, especially when you only add more ambiguity to the existing murk. In any case, not everyone who complains of depression actually has it, although—as pointed out in the incisive analysis *Schizophrenia: Medical Diagnosis or Moral Verdict?*—"clinicians who hold professional status through claiming the ability to find illness will, not unexpectedly, find illness" (18). But misdiagnosis is always a possibility, as shown by the five hundred patients who needed an average of eight years and 3.3 doctors to get their ultimate label of bipolar disorder (19).

Another concern is the fact that not everyone in treatment is equally depressed, even if they share the same designation. But to make a stronger point, Jamison collapses the spectrum of possibilities, jumbling together those who only received talk therapy with those who took mood-altering medications (of any variety or strength), and those who were hospitalized.

There are several other issues that should have been addressed in her discussion section, like the possibility that there might be perfectly healthy award winners in the world, or that her participants might have signed on because they wanted private attention from an admiring psychologist, thereby skewing the group toward the more actively unhappy.

It doesn't detract from a study to mention any external variables that might affect its outcome—in fact, it is expected. But Jamison keeps asserting that "artists and writers represent a group at high risk for affective illness" (20), as if she provides solid scientific backing for that idea. Both this and Andreasen's study continue to be advertised this way. In 2010, Jamison reaffirmed her certainty in her liner notes to a CD as well as in her onstage remarks at its launch.

The Runaway Train

THE "NEWS" ABOUT damaged creatives took off fast and far, despite an early and scathing critique by an eminently credible source. As described in chapter 1, Rothenberg spent twenty-five years guiding a research team through a broad range of scientific inquiry into the creative mind. It's worth repeating that after all that time and effort, only one thing reliably distinguished the creative person: the motivation to create (21). Not a mood disorder in sight.

But Rothenberg knew what people preferred to hear. As he points out, "The need to believe in a connection between creativity and madness appears to be so strong that affirmations are welcomed and treated rather uncritically." Rothenberg supplies some of that missing criticism by calling Andreasen's creativity criteria "inexplicit and misleading" and by finding Jamison's sample selection and hypothesis testing "questionable" with numbers "far too small to draw adequate conclusions." He cautions against trusting their results:

> Elation and disappointment have long been considered the re-
> ward and bane, respectively, of creative effort and achievement
> ... The belief that these fluctuations intrinsically reflect, or re-
> sult from, illness is conjectural and requires rigorous evidence
> for support. (22)

In his view, neither Andreasen nor Jamison provided this kind of evidence. And it's still missing, to this day.

Jamison retaliates by accusing the veteran Harvard psychiatrist Rothenberg of naïveté, or "a lack of appreciation for the subtlety, complexity, and fluctuation in the symptom patterns of manic-depressive and depressive illness, as well as insufficient awareness of the cyclic or episodic nature of these disorders" (23). She blames similar ignorance for Juda's repudiation of the genius and insanity connection, criticizing her "confusion" between schizophrenia and bipolar disorder as well as her "inadequate diagnostic methods," as if Jamison's own were impeccable (24).

Given this tradition of killing the messenger, it's no surprise that when her 2004 book got a negative write-up in the *New York Times*, Jamison launched an ad hominem attack on the reviewer:

> Daphne Merkin, who reviewed my book *Exuberance: The Pas-
> sion for Life* (Dec. 5) is an avowed masochist who has written
> exhaustively about the pleasures of pain and the miseries of her
> existence. Perhaps someone at the *Times* thought it clever to have
> such a relentlessly joyless person review a book about exuber-
> ance, but the resulting review was as predictable as it was unfair.

The newspaper ran her letter along with Merkin's reply:

> Kay Jamison's insultingly reductionistic characterization of both
> my work and my life in no way offers a substantive challenge
> to what was a thoughtful, if critical, review. The fact that the
> author sees fit to defend her effort with a scurrilous attack on

the reviewer is less in keeping with intellectual discussion than with the mud-throwing tactics of the playground. Perhaps she should aim her sights higher all around. (25)

Yet however shaky Jamison's methods may be, her message is vigorous—there are no qualifications when she informs the creative community of their fate. She told the Writers' Guild "there is a lot of science, there is a lot known," and "*we know* the natural course of the illness . . . *we know* how very, very genetic it is." Certain doom awaits the less afflicted as well, since "hypomania is more dangerous in a way because it is more functioning" (26).

Such confident assertions prime the public to accept other exaggerations, like the self-help author's casual, unreferenced "news" that writers are ten to forty times more likely to be manic-depressive than the rest of the population (27), and the *Harvard Mental Health Letter*'s claim about the "well-known association" between manic depression and creativity, which apparently needs no supportive references at all (28). But if there is such a close and well-known association between creativity and manic depression, which is so "very, very genetic," how do we explain four generations of Hemingway suicides and only one Pulitzer Prize?

Musicians learned of their fate during a broadcast from Lincoln Center when Jamison referred to "the huge body of scientific evidence" that shows "most creative composers . . . in fact suffer disproportionately from depression and manic depression." (Huge? Most? Fact?) Six years later, this "huge body of scientific evidence" becomes "surprisingly large" (29). Finally, in a dismaying "Et tu, Brute?" moment, other creativity experts insist that Ludwig, Andreasen, and Jamison have all provided "solid evidence" of the "unusually susceptible" creative (30).

That Famous List

THE BIBLE OF the mad genius movement is Jamison's 1993 *Touched with Fire: Manic-Depressive Illness and the Artistic Temperament*. Sprawling, visceral, and frequently bewildering, the book relies so heavily on poetic descriptions that its first words are Byron's—"We of the craft are all crazy"—and the last page is virtually his as well. Despite the book's frequent use as a scientific reference, Jamison did not set out to write one:

> The main purpose of this book is to make a literary, biographical, and scientific association, not to say actual overlap, between two temperaments—the artistic and the manic-depressive. (31)

Jamison's relegation of "scientific" to third place helps justify the flood of fuzzy assertions that drench her pages. But given her certainty and clout, the public has no reason to doubt her book's credibility—especially when such cultural trail markers as Amazon.com recommend it "very highly" as the definitive answer to "the age-old question of whether psychological suffering is an essential component of artistic creativity."

This online testament is followed by lavish praise from customers, including one bipolar who was thrilled to learn about her own "haunted gift for brilliance" and many who were delighted to find themselves in the company of genius.

This company, listed in Appendix B of *Fire*, is the book's most popular section. It contains Jamison's selection of 166 long-dead writers, artists, and composers with "probable cyclothymia, major depression, or manic depression," although "probable" tends to drop off whenever the list is cited.

There is also some confusion about how the list was originally assembled. On the occasions when Jamison shares her reasons for anointing a particular creative, they tend to come from gossip and circumstantial evidence; sometimes, as with Michelangelo, there is no explanation at all. Once again, the more detailed critique waits elsewhere (32). What follows are a few examples of geniuses who made the cut, and why.

Unquestionably, the great Romantic poet Samuel Coleridge was addicted to opium; everyone knows he wrote his masterpiece *Kubla Khan* in a druggy haze, and probably the spooky *Rime of the Ancient Mariner* as well. But those who use this to "prove" his madness overlook two important facts: one, that Coleridge suffered terribly from rheumatism and gout, and two, in those days opium, mixed with alcohol into a potent tonic called laudanum, was widely prescribed as a painkiller (and had been since the 1600s).

There was no knowledge or fear of addiction back then. In fact, laudanum was considered so harmless that it was also used as a cough suppressant. But Jamison knows that Coleridge "chose" to use opium "for relief from his mental perturbance and black moods" (33). She also bipolarizes Ralph Waldo Emerson, that famously serene and nature-loving philosopher, by claiming he shared Coleridge's "cosmic temperament." Perhaps this implies some manic grandiosity, but Jamison doesn't explain (34).

Fellow Romantic poet William Blake is there too, mostly because of his lifelong spiritual leanings—in childhood he claimed to see angels, and later had ongoing communication with his dead brother, Robert. This stands as proof of pathology even though he knew the dialogue was only in his memory and imagination:

> Thirteen years ago, I lost a brother, and with his spirit I converse daily and hourly in the spirit, and see him in my remembrance, in the regions of my imagination. Forgive me for expressing to you my enthusiasm, which I wish all to partake of, since it is to me a source of immortal joy, even in this world. (35)

Many bereaved people find comfort in such imaginary dialogue—are they all bipolar? A talented composer and engraver as well as poet, Blake created an elaborate mythology to illustrate his work. This powerful imagery helped reinforce that crazy creative aura, despite the fact that he was steadily productive throughout his long life and widely admired for his "remarkable sweetness, simplicity, and charm" (36). Others find the ultimate sign of reckless bipolarity in his most famous sentiment: "I must create a system, or be enslaved by another man's" (37).

Musicians are not exempt. Jamison includes composer Cole Porter in the list without noting that both his legs were crushed by a riding accident in 1937, and he endured thirty operations in the next three decades, none of which relieved his pain. This might have caused a mood swing or two. But even when list members' physical ailments are acknowledged in a footnote (Porter is mentioned without specifying the nature of his), Jamison is sure that the mental disorders preceded the physical, and stood on their own as "independently existing" entities (38).

When psychiatrist Storr died in 2001, his obituary threw more kindling on the *Fire*:

> A close friend of Kay Redfield Jamison, he was fascinated by the history of the many artists, writers and musicians whose creative drive had come from their own mental illnesses, especially depression and manic depression. The list of these is numerous and is documented in Jamison's 1993 book, *Touched with Fire*. (39)

Well . . . not quite. The fact is that this list is only printed—as opposed to actually documented—and the claim that creative drive "comes from" mental illness is a stretch of Guinness Book proportions, at best. But these statements pop up in all kinds of unexpected places—and the more casual they are, the more credibility they add to the list.

Ludwig: Rumors of Resolution

IN HIS BOOK *The Price of Greatness: Resolving the Creativity and Madness Controversy* (1995), psychiatrist Arnold Ludwig sifts the lives of 1,004 famous people for the common seeds of eminence. *Price* is another favorite of myth advocates who are too busy or otherwise disinclined to read original works, since the title itself telegraphs the verdict. The only problem is that the book is inconclusive and contradictory, and actually resolves nothing at all.

Ludwig studied *New York Times* biographies of eminent people between 1960 and 1990, culling formative factors like broken homes, birth order, and death or alleged mental illness of parents, along with others of his own invention. Like Andreasen and Jamison, he was the sole judge of his sample, with all the attendant drawbacks; as psychologists Silvia and Kaufman caution in their survey of the creativity and madness literature,

> If one person can pick the subject, choose the standard for diagnosing symptoms, assess all of the variables, and draw the conclusions, then the method is simply too impressionistic and subjective. (40)

But Ludwig's fifty-five pages of elaborate charts and graphs are convincing all by themselves, just so long as you don't examine their content too closely. Examples include the head-scratching variables of "nonconformity," "marked esthetic interests in family members," and "anger at mother," which are left undefined and their measurement unspecified.

One big hiccup is the way Ludwig builds his entire argument on the supposed objectivity of a thousand different biographers. Another problem is his equating of artistic creativity with social, athletic, scientific, military, and political eminence. People are famous for all kinds of reasons, and while the capacity to make lasting social contributions is one form of creativity, it seems odd to fold labor leader Samuel Gompers and Winston Churchill into the mix with Amelia Earhart, and weigh their psychology together with that of Harry Houdini and Marvin Gaye.

It doesn't matter that this same practice was followed by those nineteenth-century genius researchers; it still presumes an unlikely homogeneity that throws the whole enterprise into question.

Again, the more detailed critique lies elsewhere (41), but the book's flavor is obvious from just a few bites. For example, Ludwig states that musical entertainers are "relatively free from depression," but two sentences later, claims they are also "more likely to attempt suicide." While discussing parental loss, he evokes something called the "Phaethon complex," which manages to include both "reckless-ness in seeking love and attention" as well as "isolation and reserve." Time-traveling back to Lombroso and the phrenologists, Ludwig also contemplates Andy Warhol's pale skin and the "large bony pro-tuberances" on Debussy's forehead, although he fails to connect such physical anomalies with eminence.

Considering that *Price* is widely cited as strong support for the mad genius myth, it's surprising that Ludwig actually *debunks* it when he writes that "mental illness does not seem necessary for exceptional achievement." He also notes that the creative professions "have substan-tial percentages of persons who are emotionally stable throughout their lives, **showing that mental illness is not essential for artistic success**" (42, emphasis mine). So why is this book considered proof that it is?

The most obvious reason is that, once again, nobody's read it. In this case, the title seems to supply the answer by itself, since "the price of greatness" confirms that genius is psychologically expensive, while "resolving the creativity and madness controversy" suggests that the jury is in, sentence has been pronounced, and we can all go home. But the truth is that both concepts remain just as slippery as ever.

Yelling "Crazy" in a Crowded Concert Hall

FOR MY MONEY, the most egregious exploitation of the mad genius myth is the series of concerts that began in 1988, when Jamison produced a Kennedy Center concert to "honor" four allegedly bipolar compos-ers. Their diagnoses were "proven" by their own compositions, as the National Symphony played their faster sections to show their mania, and the slower ones to demonstrate their depression.

Turned into a documentary called *Moods and Music* and nation-ally broadcast on PBS in November 1989, the video features works by

Berlioz, Schumann, Wolf, and Handel rendered by the orchestra and the superb mezzo-soprano Ruby Hinds, whose dramatic facial contortions magnify the musical contrast between ecstasy and despair. The narrator is actor Louis Jourdan (star of the 1958 movie *Gigi*), whose doleful brown eyes enhance the tragic message he brings. Jamison also appears to spray-paint the enterprise in scientific semigloss.

In many ways, this video is a microcosm of the mad genius campaign: all that questionable science intoned with such dark conviction, and so much distortion of the creative life. Here Handel becomes bipolar because his long periods of productivity were "broken" by the times when he was inactive; like other researchers, Jamison represents creativity as a steady-state process where any spikes or lulls must be caused by some mental aberration.

Handel's alleged "mania" is evident in the legendary speed with which he wrote his *Messiah*—reportedly in three weeks "of intense creative energy" (43). This too is evidence of pathology, especially when nobody wonders whether Handel was rushing to meet a fast-approaching commission deadline. As it turns out, his contemporaries Bach and Telemann were known to write at a similar brisk pace, and neither of them is considered mentally disordered

Moreover, in examining the records and reports of the time, psychiatrist William Frosch writes, "Except in relation to his episodes of physical difficulty [palsy and blindness, both affecting his ability to play and compose], I do not find contemporaneous evidence of significant mood swings . . . primary depression or mania." Frosch asks, "If there is little real evidence of either cyclothymia or major affective illness, how are we to understand such claims by modern writers?" Helpfully answering his own question, he cites "creeping inaccuracies" of history as well as the changing meaning of "genius" itself (44).

The video goes on to offer a flowchart of Schumann's output, with frowning attention paid to the year 1840, when he wrote almost 150 songs—a clear sign of mania! Yes, Robert Schumann did throw himself into the Rhine and spent his last years in an asylum, but this behavior has also been linked to the maddening effects of tertiary syphilis, which also killed Wolf (45). Here, we'll borrow Simonton's excellent question: "Is it fair to brand a luminary as 'nuts' when the brain has been taken over by some virus or bacterium?" (46). Many would say no—but that doesn't keep it from happening.

Soon Byron crashes the party, ostensibly because Manfred, the supernatural hero of one of his poems, inspired Schumann's 1852 "Overture to Manfred." But Byron's cameo enables Jamison to import his histrionic descriptions of creative torment into her discussion of what motivates these musicians.

Gustav Mahler is labeled agoraphobic as well as manic-depressive. We are not told that his crippling anxiety and withdrawal began after his beloved daughter died and he learned he had heart disease; nor is it ever mentioned that he had to bury ten of his siblings. The video's "proof" of Wolf's pathology is the fact that he wrote both a happy and sad song in the same day, which are performed together to illustrate his mood disorder. His history of progressive paralysis, which strongly suggests syphilis, is not part of his portrait (47).

Berlioz is said to diagnose himself with his "uncannily clinical descriptions of his moods," such as his remark that "sensible people have no idea what it is to have this intense consciousness of simply being alive" (that couldn't be creative joy, could it?). We're also told that a sure sign of his depression is telling his father that he couldn't live without music, which describes nearly everybody I know. Meanwhile, the orchestra demonstrates his manic side by furiously sawing and blowing its way through his "Damnation of Faust."

The video continues with an animated graph to emphasize the gravity of bipolar disorder. In a dramatic comparison of suicide rates among depressed versus non-depressed individuals, the first bar zooms past the second to depict a staggering imbalance of seventy-five to one. This is a stunning image unless you consider the obvious: how often do happy people commit suicide?

The spectacle finally ends with the claim that "the scientific and biographical evidence for a link between artistic creativity and mood disorders is incontrovertible." This is patently false, as well as typical.

But the public eats it up, so it's not going to stop: the concert was re-created by the Mansfield (Ohio) Symphony, with Jamison as featured speaker (October 27, 2007), and the Baltimore Symphony was planning to "honor" Schumann in 2011. Jamison participated in an August 2011 music festival at Bard College in Annandale-on-Hudson, New York; the program was called "White Nights–Dark Mornings: Creativity, Depression, and Addiction" and targeted Jean Sibelius, Edvard Grieg, and Alma Mahler, none of whom is on her original "crazy" list.

Jamison's uniquely passionate advocacy for the mad genius has shown such a "sovereign disregard for evidence" (48) that it seems personal, reprising the "faces in a cloud" discussion in chapter 1. She may be trying to glamorize her own bipolar disorder, as described in her 1995 memoir, which would explain both her poeticizing of the problem and her consuming drive to equate it with genius.

At the very least, Jamison insists it's a useful tool: "It is my perspective that the illness itself, in the context of a creative mind, can at certain times create a very definite advantage for the artist" (49). And in 2002, advantage rose to necessity when she referred to "the **beholdenness** of certain kinds of creative work to the manic and melancholic temperaments" (50, emphasis mine).

I'm sure Jamison's disclosure has helped many people who share her diagnosis. But exalting the disorder is something else entirely:

> I have often asked myself whether, given the choice, I would choose to have manic-depressive illness . . . Strangely enough, I think I would choose to have it . . . I honestly believe that, as a result of it, I have felt more things, more deeply; had more experiences, more intensely; loved more, and have been more loved . . . But normal or manic I have run faster, thought faster, and loved faster than most I know. (51)

Perhaps it makes it easier to confer that diagnosis on others—no matter how sparse the evidence—when it's viewed as such a blessing. But not everyone considers it such welcome news.

SIX

Blunt Tools and Slippery Slopes

I can answer you in two words: im-possible.

~ Samuel Goldwyn

THE PREVIOUS CHAPTER DISMANTLED THE most popular evidence for the creativity and madness link. This one explains why legitimate answers will never be found: mad genius research has too many inherent obstacles to be definitive, no matter how devoted or meticulous the seeker may be.

To begin with , those definition and measurement problems discussed in part 1 are scientifically insurmountable. It's impossible to take two slippery, amorphous variables and determine if, how, and where they interact. It's like trying to get two clumps of jello to stick together (1).

But the intrepid explorer who wants to press on anyway will come upon other formidable blocks in the road, like the quality of information mad genius advocates keep using to make their point. In addition to quoting the famous trio discussed in the previous chapter, supporters of the myth tend to mine their "evidence" from three other main quarries:

1. The **words of antiquity**, which lend that timeless tremor

of "truth" to any concept, and suggest that someone will eventually prove what has always been "known"

2. The **melodramatic kvetching of famous poets** about the torment they endure in the service of their creative gift

3. The **primitive theories of nineteenth-century researchers**, whose names are collected to imply a long scientific pedigree for the mad genius idea, but whose actual writings are rarely specified, given how ludicrous most of them are

Even if researchers take a more rigorous approach—say, conducting empirical studies of living people—serious methodological problems still stand between them and their proof. What follows now are some of the biggest.

Sampling, Self-Report, and Sucking Up

THE GOLD STANDARD of sampling is to gather participants randomly, thus lowering the risk of stacking the deck with those most likely to prove the case. In contrast, the most influential studies have used participants who are handpicked and of the same gender, race, and age, all of which restricts the application of results.

Another popular tactic is to gather up a great crowd from wildly different fields and backgrounds and consider them together just because they're all famous. Some authors study their own patients or those they happen to know, compounding the risk of experimenter bias that dogs every study, regardless of its focus.

For instance, results can be nudged in the desired direction by the order and phrasing of research questions (2). Bias lurks at the other end too, since it's well-known that whenever questionnaires are mailed out, the response rate is typically low. In the DRADA membership survey discussed in chapter 5, only 27 percent of the forms came back (3).

This automatically restricts the sample to those with the strongest personal motivation to participate. And who'd be more eager to join a mad genius expedition than those who suspect they qualify on one or both counts, and are looking for answers? Such self-selection can easily twist a survey's results, leading to erroneous conclusions.

Bias is also unavoidable in "live" studies, when the researcher and subject are together in real time. First of all, there's a natural human impulse to "do well" in an interview by giving the examiners what they're looking for. And if writers are asked about creativity, they may be happy to expound on the process while increasing its drama by a decibel or two.

Natural human impulses apply to researchers too, making them nod and smile and perhaps scribble more notes when they hear material they know will be useful. Despite their best attempts to be neutral, their body language can telegraph enthusiasm, alerting the interviewee as to which topics and attitudes are most welcome. This can shape the dialogue as well as the study's outcome.

So can the proclivity for sucking up to authority figures, especially when participants are psychology students, that large, captive, and grade-dependent population; even if the research is anonymous, some will always be guided by the desire to please. Extraneous factors also leak into people's self-descriptions, given the common tendency to tweak reality to confirm or enhance one's self-image, and to report what they assume they're *supposed to* think and feel, which might be far from the truth (4).

Compounding the challenge of self-report is the memory problem. Recollections can be fallible. Sometimes feelings and experiences emerge only if they're asked about them; others might be constructed just for the occasion. And psychologists continue to disagree over the phenomenon of false memory, or the power of outside suggestion in "helping" people recall things that never happened.

Scientific precision is always compromised when researchers rely so heavily on what people say about their own attitudes, moods, and behaviors, rather than observing these things directly. But since self-report is so easy to collect, it will always be the favorite tool in the shed.

Insignificance and Incomplete Maps

Once a study is done and disseminated, its value can be artificially inflated by the common misunderstanding of one word: "significance." In research this refers to the contribution of chance, or the probability that a study's findings are not a mere fluke or coincidence—*not* that they are particularly noteworthy.

As such, the news that a "significant difference" has been found does not mean it's remarkable or even especially useful. But the word "significant" often generates more attention and respect than the findings actually deserve. It's good to keep this in mind when reading breathless media bulletins from the research front.

The one report that could contribute something truly meaningful rarely comes. That would be news of a successful replication: that someone closely copied the methodology of a prior study, used it on the same kind of population, and got virtually the same results. Every "replica" adds credibility and weight to the original findings, making it more likely that something real is being measured or observed. Unfortunately, "replication is too seldom practiced in any research" (5).

This is primarily because journals and popular science media are loathe to print what seems like "old" news. And most researchers would rather claim their own mountain than plant a second flag on somebody else's. Some creativity experts have solved this problem by degrading the value of replication altogether, claiming that combining all the unmatched studies produces a more convincing result. This is false but clever, since it instantly legitimizes decades of weak research simply by lowering the bar.

Another area that brims with false confidence is genetics. Some mad genius advocates not only claim that their evidence is "scientific"—which it isn't—but that it also has strong genetic backing, which, so far, is impossible. More than ten years after the human genome was mapped, there's still no successful linkage of any disease to its genetic endowment.

The term "mapping" is misleading by itself, since it implies that specific areas of function and dysfunction have been identified as clearly as blue and red states. Instead, the only territory that's clear is the genetic sequence—which proteins make up which genes, and in what order—not what the genes actually *do*. The fact that about 24,000 genes have been "identified" doesn't mean that their functions are understood. But then the field of psychiatric genetics is known to be fraught with misrepresentation (6) and sensationalist claims that pass for evidence (7).

The official genome website (http://genomics.energy.gov) is quite clear that it's still not possible to predict who is susceptible to which disease. And this includes tangible entities like cancer and diabetes, not vague and invisible concepts like creativity and madness. Even the STEP-BD study, which completed its original mandate in 2005, continues to collect blood samples in its own quest for the genetic basis of bipolar disorder.

Meanwhile, as of this writing, Columbia University is actively soliciting participants—particularly families—for their own bipolar genetic study with the New York State Psychiatric Institute. Their invitation concedes the current state of knowledge: that the responsible genes have *not* been isolated, and that bipolar disorder may not be caused by the same gene(s) in all individuals—in other words, we do not know what's behind it, and whatever it is might vary among different people anyway. Columbia is admirably frank about how little is actually known (8).

In contrast, many mad genius advocates refer to genetic connections as if they were already found and authenticated. In her *Moods and Music* video, for instance, Jamison refers to the "indisputable scientific evidence that it's genetic, and runs in families." But instead of certainty, there's just a dizzying proliferation of alphabet candidates like CACNA1C or CHRNA7 or P14K2B. As described in a recent research summary:

> We now know that we will not find one specific gene or a few
> specific genes for BD [bipolar disorder]. We may have to settle

for a scenario where we can only sufficiently characterize the joint effect of several hundreds or even thousands of genes on disease presentation. (9)

Given the tradition of commercial exaggeration and quick fixes for this diagnosis, it's not surprising that the public is being offered a "bipolar spit test" to measure their DNA at home.

Yet even an unmistakable connection between specific genes and psychological disorders would still not tell the whole story. Social factors will always churn up the mix; after all, poverty also runs in families, but that doesn't make it genetic.

Modeling will always have a huge impact on family resemblance. People who restrict themselves to genetic explanations miss the fact that the young learn appropriate mood displays from their elders, just as they watch and absorb other customs of behavior and attitude. A young man ricochets between dark sulks and grandiose rants because his favorite uncle acts the same way; in another family, tantrums are the customary way to communicate simple frustration. Is this disordered emotionality or merely stylistic? Either way, it's a blend of inheritance and learning.

Keep Those Bell Bottoms

THAT NATURE/NURTURE QUESTION is one of the most heated debates in all of psychology—it certainly provoked long and lively arguments in every class I ever taught. Most students had surprisingly visceral opinions as to whether genetics or environment was more influential in shaping human behavior, but that was before the advent of "epigenetics," which officially accommodates them both.

I knew I should've kept my old bell-bottom jeans from the '60s: wait long enough, and every fashion will return. Epigenetics is actually a reincarnation of Jean-Baptiste Lamarck's Theory of Acquired Characteristics, which first appeared in the early 1800s. This theory held that acquired traits could be inherited—the classic example being giraffes who stretch their necks to reach the highest branches and then pass this new length on to their offspring. I remember my eighth-grade science teacher making fun of this idea, since Darwin's dominant theory made Lamarck's seem so unlikely.

But here we are, four decades later—bell bottoms are back and so is the interaction between environment and DNA. Epigenetic theory states that factors such as upbringing, diet, living conditions, toxins, and stress all create "biochemical markers" that affect whether a gene will be active or silent—markers that may well be heritable. Lamarck would be delighted and Lombroso would be horrified to hear that "genes are ruled by the environment," and "predisposition is not destiny" (10).

By now, it should be obvious that, despite all the ongoing study and debate, nobody can say for sure that aberrant behavior, artistic talent, or anything else is caused by a particular gene or group of genes. But for more than a century, people have been convinced that genius and madness are biologically linked and carried together through the generations. They're sure because experts keep telling them so. And they're still saying it.

For all we know, mental aberration could be a function of some physical illness that is yet to be identified. Two centuries ago, the culprit was tuberculosis—said to be "the bane of the brilliant" with a "tendency to create genius," it had a long list of prominent victims, like musician Frederick Chopin; poets John Milton, Keats, Shelley, and Elizabeth Barrett Browning; writers Goethe, Hawthorne, Voltaire, Emerson, Balzac, and Austen; and philosophers Kant, Spinoza, and Rousseau (11).

A more convincing case can be made for syphilis, since the later stages produce symptoms that are virtually indistinguishable from bipolar disorder. Deborah Hayden, author of *Pox: Genius, Madness, and the Mysteries of Syphilis* (2003), calls it "The Great Imitator," and documents its signature pattern of alternating euphoria and misery, lucidity and delirium in the lives of James Joyce, Oscar Wilde, Nietzsche, Van Gogh, Hugo Wolf, and Schumann.

It was also intriguing to learn that after 1850, when Schumann had one physical complaint after another, including fainting and weakness, a Dr. Müller prescribed "eighteen cold plunges in the Rhine" (12). Is it possible that Schumann's last and most famous plunge was not suicidal at all, but rather a confused attempt to follow his doctor's orders?

Diagnosing the Dead

PERHAPS THE MOST popular technique in mad genius research—and certainly the most entertaining—is the "psychological autopsy," or the dissection of the life and work of dead geniuses in order to evaluate how crazy they were. This approach has been used by many prominent names in the field such as Lombroso, Ellis, and Nisbet; Juda, Jamison, and Ludwig; and Felix Post and Geoffrey Wills, whose indictment of forty jazz musicians will be discussed in a minute.

The work of Post resembles that of Jamison and Ludwig in that researchers often cite it without noting what he actually did. Post single-handedly scoured the biographies of 291 famous men in science, philosophy, politics, and arts for data he could transform into DSM-III diagnoses. Although he followed the tradition of focusing on mood disorders, he could not verify major depression at all and had to manipulate the diagnostic criteria for other categories because of the limitations of his biographical information. This muddies his results from the start. He also admits that

> translating the personality characteristics from their descriptions in the biographies to specific DSM traits could obviously not achieve high levels of validity and reliability in the hands of a single investigator. (13)

One wonders, then: what's the point? It's too bad that the methodology was so weak, since Post seems to support the point I'm trying to make: "Psychoses, to which an inordinate amount of attention continues to be paid, were confirmed to be even rarer in 'geniuses' than in members of the general population" (14). Given his study's limitations, it must be offered as an opinion, rather than an empirical result.

But Post keeps getting pulled into the mad genius parade and is often pushed to the front of it. This is probably because he used that popular autopsy method, since he actually rejects the myth.

The method itself is imprecise and conjectural: producing "more insults than insights," it "can reach a degree of distorted judgment that has few parallels in the works of historians" (15). There's certainly a lot of Olympic-level straining to make a point. For example, Jamison finds evidence of bipolar disorder in someone's interest in spiritualism, as well as in other people's opinions and garden-variety gossip—"thought by others to have had at least a trace of insanity." And the qualification implicit in "possibly transient hypomanic episodes" makes that "evidence" virtually meaningless (16).

Diagnoses are usually based on subjects' letters (from and to them), as well as on observations from friends, family members, and even strangers. These sources are as suspect as any form of self-report, and just as vulnerable to the vagaries of personal relationships; moreover, one argument can produce a distorted portrait that resonates through the centuries. Although these secondary sources are prone to self-serving distortions—and swerve deep into the territory of gossip and hearsay—researchers treat their insights as respectfully as if they were solid data:

> These judgments may come from experienced psychiatrists, yet the evaluations are often based on skimpy information about symptoms . . . many of these diagnoses would not stand up in a court of law. (17)

Asylum stays are always a bonus. If mad genius advocates discover that creative people were ever hospitalized, they pounce on it as ultimate proof of their insanity. What they overlook is the fact that, in the early days of psychiatry, any of the following items could get you committed:

Asthma, sunstroke, intemperance, business nerves, jealousy
Parents were cousins
Seduction and disappointment
Cold, indigestion, carbonic acid gas, carbuncle
Gathering in the head, softening of the brain, overaction of the mind
Bad habits, novel reading, egotism, vicious vices in early life
Bad company, doubt about mother's ancestors
Laziness
Women [dealing with, not being one]

This list was found in the dusty records of "The Lunatic Asylum West of the Alleghenys" in West Virginia; later called Weston State Hospital, it admitted its first patients in 1864. Although it closed 150 years later, you can still sign up for a "Haunted Hospital Tour" that includes a bonus hayride (18).

These days, with all the options for voluntary commitment in cushy quarters, any exhausted person with good insurance or sufficient cash can take a private rest without signifying any permanent mental derailment. It's the ideal place for celebrities to wait out their latest scandal, while attributing any egregious misbehavior to some psychiatric syndrome or other (this is one step removed from "the devil made me do it"). But future researchers can label them mentally "ill" just because they spent time there, whatever the actual circumstances may have been.

The Goldwater Rule

MAD GENIUS FANS also prefer to ignore all the great individuals who have managed to be exceptional without being disordered. Jamison's Bipolar 166 is the most-cited collection of crazy creatives, but there are others:

The cumulative effect of these long lists, certainly upon the authors themselves, convinced them of the rightness of their theses. What none of them did was to look at the evidence statistically. They did not consider rates. Their attention was captured by the size of the numerator but not by that of the denominator, for they completely ignored the large numbers of sane great individuals. (19)

Even the remote diagnosis of a living person is suspect. In 1964, responding to a magazine survey, over two thousand psychiatrists who never met him pronounced Senator Barry M. Goldwater unfit to be president. After Goldwater sued the magazine, the APA issued a set of guidelines about making such conclusions and sharing them with the media. The essence of the 1973 "Goldwater rule" is this:

First, it is intellectually dishonest for a mental health professional—or any physician—to give a diagnosis without examining the patient. A professional opinion is supposed to reflect a thorough and rigorous evaluation of a patient and all relevant clinical data obtained under the protection of strict confidentiality. Anything short of that misleads the public about what constitutes accepted medical practice and invites distrust of the profession as a whole. (20)

Clearly, the rule hasn't stopped anybody. There's additional distortion when normal behavior is presented as if it were pathological. For example, Ludwig claims trumpeter Bix Beiderbecke had "mental symptoms" because he "began having increasing trouble finding his 'embouchure' with the mouthpiece [the proper playing position of lips, tongue, and teeth], and later began relying more on a derby and other devices to mute his tone in an attempt to disguise his deficiencies" (21). When I ran Ludwig's diagnosis past master trumpeter and Bix expert Randy Sandke, he said Ludwig's interpretation was "totally uninformed and specious" (22).

In any event, it's always problematic to rely so heavily on recorded biographies, since the truth can easily be twisted by a writer's desire to protect or expose his subject. This happened when biographer Robert Gutman offered this mocking interpretation of Richard Wagner's "fetishistic" love of silks and satins:

> That his skin was extremely sensitive may explain his silk chokers and underwear but hardly those quilted, shirred, bowed, laced, flowered, fringed and furred gowns he dragged through his private rooms.

Storr notes that unlike some other writers, Gutman did not idolize Wagner and thus "is not so concerned to protect him" (23).

Here's a more recent example of how the image of a dead genius can be manipulated. Peter Shaffer, author of *Amadeus* (both the 1979 play and 1984 film) admits that his Mozart is "an irritatingly distasteful little fellow with few redeeming qualities." He deliberately drew him that way to create a dramatic rationale for Salieri's intense jealousy and hatred (24), which were central to his plot. As a result, millions of people got their idea of the "real" Mozart from actor Tom Hulce's outrageous portrayal—an extra bonus for the mad genius crowd, for whom a sensible Mozart would never do.

Poor Wolfgang has also been posthumously diagnosed with Tourette's syndrome because of his "roguish playfulness," use of obscenity, and preference for ca-ca jokes. The involuntary motor tics that are the true hallmarks of the disease—and would have been obvious to those around him, including his audiences—are not mentioned (25). It's just one more diagnostic shot in the dark.

And finally, ever chasing that bipolar connection, Jamison quotes one author who claims Mozart had manic-depressive "tendencies," as well as unnamed others "who **feel** that Mozart had manic depression" (26, emphasis mine). There is no need to bring up Mozart's actual behavior when the experts are so intuitively convinced. Although this happens with other creatives, it especially irks me when musicians are nailed to the dissection board, and cannot answer for themselves, as the next section will show.

The Battle of Britain

HERE'S YET ANOTHER example of the determination to pin the "mad genius" tail on the creative donkey. I once had a small skirmish across the pond in the *British Journal of Psychiatry* (BJP). Several musician friends had pointed me to "Forty Lives in the Bebop Business," an article by psychologist Geoffrey Wills, in which he "finds" (or implies) psychopathology in virtually every great player of the bebop era. This impression of universal pathology is reinforced by a table that lists all forty musicians and the instruments they played; coming right after another table of mood-disordered players, it implies that all forty are somehow disturbed as well. There's no practical reason to identify each man's instrument except to get all those names in front of the reader—in an article about musician pathology, this table is a subliminal visual statement that they all qualify.

There's more explicit silliness, however. Much like Ludwig's diagnosis of Bix, Wills finds obsessive-compulsive disorder (OCD) in saxophonist John Coltrane's ongoing search for the perfect mouthpiece and his "excessive practicing" (this last "symptom" prompted sustained laughter from every musician who heard it). The kindest explanation is that since Wills is a drummer, he might not fully appreciate how central the perfect mouthpiece is to a horn player.

But there's no excuse to denigrate Coltrane's famous spiritual questing as another OCD symptom because it involved "constant" exploration (27). It's also pushing it to note the "severe learning difficulties" of pianist Errol Garner's twin brother, as if this proved there was something pathological about Errol. Finally, is it fair for Wills to include saxophonist Gerry Mulligan in the mood-disordered list when he also indicates that it's "due to hypoglycaemia" (28)?

Perhaps the most disingenuous moment comes when Wills shoehorns the famously sane and good-natured Dizzy Gillespie into the discussion because Diz recalled being beaten by his father—even though this was hardly unusual paternal behavior for that time. While neither

Garner nor Gillespie gets a specific diagnosis, their listing among those who do implies that they were "troubled beboppers" as well.

Some readers who continue to the very end may get confused. In discussing "non-pathological sample characteristics," Wills seems to reverse himself when he notes that Miles Davis—whom he earlier diagnosed with addiction, mood disorder with depressive features, and psychosis—actually overcame his problems to become "very successful and highly respected" (29). This is admirable, if rather baffling, in context. In fact, the whole article is a bit of a head-scratcher.

When the BJP printed my criticism of Wills's article and his reliance on Jamison, Andreasen, and Ludwig, the transatlantic feathers began to fly. Wills defended Jamison's *Fire* as a fount of credible information, and characterized the psychological autopsy as "a legitimate exercise if one follows rigorous guidelines as laid down, for instance, in the scholarly work of Runyan (1982)" (30).

Well, I looked up those "rigorous guidelines," and found two Runyan articles published about the same time. I read the more mainstream piece first because its title seemed directly relevant: "Why Did Van Gogh Cut Off His Ear?: The Problem of Alternative Explanations in Psychobiography." Here Runyan ponders the difficulty of arriving at clear interpretations of past events when so many are possible, and comes up with thirteen separate psychodynamic reasons for Van Gogh's slicing of his ear.

These include the ear as phallic symbol, because he was conflicted over his homosexual impulses toward Gauguin, or he may have been copying a bullfighter or Jack the Ripper, who was in the news at the time. Van Gogh might have been acting out a scene from the Biblical Garden of Gethsemane or conjuring the older brother who died, with his ear lobe representing a baby. Runyan acknowledges the dilemma of choosing among them and concludes that even with the best of efforts, more than one explanation may remain (31). If this constitutes rigorous guidelines, I will eat my dog's dinner. Twice.

So I tried Runyan's other article, where he does enumerate many weaknesses of the case study method and recommends caution in interpreting subjective reports. But his only specific remedy is this: "a quasijudicial or adversarial procedure . . . in which the evidence and arguments in case studies are subject to critical examination and reformulation" (32). There's no sign that anyone in this field has followed this excellent advice—including Wills.

I felt like I'd been sent in pursuit of one of Alfred Hitchcock's "McGuffins," his term for an intriguing plot twist that deliberately distracts the audience from the true culprits. In any case, there's no sign that Wills subjected his ideas to any special quasijudicial procedure except submitting them for publication and the usual vetting by peer reviewers.

In response to my criticism, Wills accused me of resurrecting the outdated "anti-psychiatry" view of the '60s and '70s, claiming I got my naïve views from R. D. Laing, the renegade psychiatrist who painted the madman as a courageous visionary. "Have we not moved on since then?" he sighs (33).

The BJP kindly printed my full answer to that challenge, which I am happy to share:

> As far as my concerns being passé—reflecting the "anti-psychiatry" movement of the '60s and '70s—the news is that objection to reckless labeling never disappeared. It's actually growing, particularly in the U.S., where even the general public has noticed the link between elastic diagnoses and pharmaceutical profits. **I make no apologies for believing creative people to be heroic, especially these days, when so many assume they are mentally disabled, thanks to all this wobbly pseudoscience.** (34, emphasis doubly mine)

This turned out to be the last word, since Wills went silent after that.

But other professionals are so preoccupied with musical madness that they keep pushing the mute button on reality. When composer Igor Stravinsky abruptly changed his style after premiering "The Rite of Spring," Storr said it was because his "obsessional nature" was frightened by the "Dionysian" impulses he had discovered in himself, which in turn activated "his fear of loss of control" (35).

What Storr neglected to mention was the most famous riot in musical history. During Spring's 1913 Paris debut, the audience was so agitated by its radically discordant sounds that they ended up fighting each other in the aisles and out into the street. This alone could explain Stravinsky's decision to write "safer" music for the rest of his life.

Playing devil's advocate for a moment, let's say a gifted musician is obviously troubled. Let's even agree to call it "bipolar disorder." But the story is still incomplete, since nobody knows how, or even whether, this directly connects to his talent. Do his psychological problems inspire his creativity—or have nothing to do with it at all?

Only one thing is absolutely sure in this area, and it's this: anyone who believes that a particular creative is disturbed will always find some historical nugget to "prove" it. This is despite any expert opinions to the contrary, such as that of psychiatrist William Frosch, who concluded his extensive study of the area with this: "That there is a psychology of musical creativity, I do not doubt. That there is a pathology to it, I find no compelling evidence" (36).

Quantifying History

Historiometry uses a quantitative approach to understanding exceptional individuals. The term was coined in 1909 by biologist and eugenicist Frederick Woods; believing that "history stands somewhere between . . . the quagmire of complete falsehood and heights of perfect truth," he was looking for more reliable ways to analyze the great, whether living or dead.

Woods applied mathematical principles to evaluating famous achievers that he collected from biographical dictionaries and volumes of *Who's Who in America*. For example, Woods claimed that Massachusetts generated a disproportionate share of eminent men, while Virginia should have produced more, "given its large white population" (37).

Woods's ideas are more fully developed by Simonton in his *Psychology, Science & History* (1990). Unlike the psychological autopsists who comb biographies for tattletale tidbits to confirm their expectations, "historiometrics feeds on historical facts ... with relatively little use for narrative" (38). The problem is that many facts are only frozen bits of narrative, making historiometry as vulnerable to conjecture and personal agenda as a fretful letter from a creative's mother.

It does seem precise, however, when the IQs of Beethoven, Rembrandt, and Copernicus are reported as if these scores were established by the usual procedures. But they weren't, since calculating someone's I(ntelligence) Q(uotient), at least according to the standard Wechsler Test for adults, requires direct questioning about vocabulary and interpretation of common sayings; there's also a performance part, where people are timed on simple tasks like block assembly and putting pictures in proper sequence to tell a story. Each subtest generates a numerical score that's used to compute the overall IQ.

But all of these scores are only meaningful when compared to the test's established norms, which were created by administering it to thousands of living people under prescribed conditions with standardized materials. So while it could be useful for argument's sake to assign a "smartness ranking" to a dead eminence, it's hardly equivalent to the modern IQ test, and cannot borrow its validity and clout.

There are also problems in the measurement of "charisma" of thirty-four world leaders, a list that Simonton adapts from an earlier author and features such names as Churchill, Nasser, Ben Gurion, Mao, Roosevelt, and Hitler. Here, a numerical value is assigned to eleven "indicators" of charisma—numbers 10 and 11 are "sexual prowess" and "women make sacrifices for leader," respectively, although no explanation is provided as to how such things are determined (39). A more popular focus is ranking U.S. presidents, since Simonton reports nine separate attempts.

His own chart compares their standing on fourteen general "personality dimensions," including "physical attractiveness," however that may be verified (again, no defining criteria are offered). Yet even when quantified, they can still be problematic—for example, a colleague measures greatness by a president's years as wartime commander in chief, although some of the wars may be ill-managed or even disastrous.

The book contains numerous examples of creative thinking, such as Simonton's "dendogram" indicating the similarity of personality among thirty-nine presidents. Since he notes that these men were "reliably assessed" earlier, you must dig up his "1986g" citation to understand what this means.

But having done that and read it carefully, I still don't understand how these individuals were actually assessed. There are no clues as to how a president gets a high score on, for example, "poise and polish," "pettiness," or "evasiveness." Instead, the article seems more focused on correlating the descriptors with each other—comparing different investigators' adjectives, which unsurprisingly overlap—than explaining what a person had to do or be to qualify for them.

Here's the kind of bold assertion that appears without explanation: "Presidents who are targets of assassination attempts, whether successful or not, score more highly on forcefulness but below average in tidiness" (40). First, how did they determine tidiness? Has somebody been in the presidential sock drawers? Next, does this mean that opinionated presidents who are sloppy dressers are more likely to be targeted than those whose pants creases are sharp? Any theory as to why? Should the Secret Service be informed?

Similarly, when Simonton reports that "more recent presidents tend to be affectionate, humorous, and natural" (41), he says nothing about how many hugs or jokes might be required and who is responsible for counting them (and what does "natural" look like, anyway?). It's all very confusing, particularly for a technique that's supposed to add precision to a famously murky area.

Finally, although I'm not usually dumb, I got lost in this: "A between-group average-linkage cluster analysis was then applied to the squared Euclidean distances between the presidents, producing the dendrogram exhibited in Figure 1" (42). I do understand that this generates a matrix of similarities, but couldn't tell how this related to the accompanying claim that five of the presidents are "highly idealistic, even self-righteous, and eminently stubborn" (43). Based on what? The investigators' categories seem to float in some "meta" land far above the people they are supposed to be describing. It seems historiometricians make their own rules:

> Investigators cannot take for granted what the unit of analysis will be, but rather they must always carefully tailor the research design to best fit the hypotheses to be tested. Historiometrics is not for those psychologists who like to play Procrustes by cutting and stretching every research question into an identical, preconceived analytical framework. (44)

But that "identical, preconceived analytical framework" is nothing less than the rules of traditional research. Psychologists don't adhere to these procedures because they are too timid or unimaginative to make up their own, but because the conventions provide common standards and language for discussing and fairly evaluating one another's work.

But as we have seen, creativity researchers can be, well, creative—dismissing the standard protocols and making up their own definitions, measurements, and procedures. In mad genius research, it seems like everyone is busy reinventing the wheel, which prevents combining their disparate studies into a strong case for anything. There's nothing wrong with proposing a fresh approach, particularly in an area that sorely needs some new ones, but I don't understand the utility of the historiometric method, which seems to reject the research tradition while selectively borrowing its credibility.

Poetic License and Licentious Poets

THE MAD GENIUS idea was born in philosophy and nursed on literature. But consider this: what other "scientific" inquiry hauls out volumes of poetry to make its case?

A favorite source is William Shakespeare, whose great, enduring art lends extra weight to everything he says, including his observations on human nature. In *A Midsummer Night's Dream*, his claim that lovers, poets, and lunatics "are of imagination all compact" is often used to "prove" the inherent kinship between artists and madmen. But nobody ever quotes the lines that follow, where he actually draws clear lines between them:

> One sees more devils than vast hell can hold,
> That is, the madman: the lover, all as frantic,
> Sees Helen's beauty in a brow of Egypt . . .
> The poet's eye, in a fine frenzy rolling,
> Doth glance from heaven to earth, from earth to
>   heaven,
> And as imagination bodies forth
> The forms of things unknown, the poet's pen
> Turns them to shapes, and gives to airy nothing
> A local habitation and a name. (45)

The worst the poet does is to scan the world and create things from his imagination. The frenzy in his eye is "fine"—active and alert, not crazed—it's only the madman and lover who are frantic and deluded, not all three.

Yet this part is overlooked, and so Shakespeare's snippet gets filed with other literary "evidence," such as everybody's favorite lines from poet and critic John Dryden: "Great wits are sure to madness near allied / And thin partitions do their bounds divide." This couplet clearly suggests that "great wits" are especially vulnerable to insanity.

But once again, the meaning shifts when the lines are restored to their original context—there, it turns out that rather than making any universal statement about exceptional talent, Dryden is only pondering the behavior of one foolish old man:

> Great wits are sure to madness near allied,
> And thin partitions do their bounds divide;

Else, why should he, with wealth and honour blest,
Refuse his age the needful hours of rest?
Punish a body which he could not please;
Bankrupt of life, yet prodigal of ease?
And all to leave what with his toil he won,
To that unfeathered two-legged thing, a son. (46)

For obvious reasons, nobody who uses those two famous lines reveals that they come from a political satire written with tongue firmly in cheek ("unfeathered two-legged thing"?). Acknowledging the humor would undermine that "thin partitions" observation, which has by now achieved the status of certified psychological insight.

There's nothing new or particularly unscrupulous about plucking things out of context—all scholars pan the literature for gleaming nuggets to enrich their case. But it's both arrogant and misleading to claim that the mad genius has a solid empirical basis, and then peddle so much poetry instead.

"Mad, bad, and dangerous to know." This was how one of his many mistresses described the poet Byron. Given his melodramatic spoutings, handsome face, and scandalous sexuality, he's always been a favorite poster boy for the mad genius idea. Van Gogh is a strong contender—although his behavior was less flagrant, he provides the best visual (that *Self-Portrait with Bandaged Ear*).

Byron complains about writing "as a torture, which I must get rid of, but never as a pleasure" (47). Jamison makes Byron emblematic of all great creatives, using his confident assertion that "we of the craft are all crazy" to open *Fire* (48). But it's quite possible that he was being deliberately outrageous.

In fact, according to his contemporary, novelist William Thackeray, "That man never wrote from the heart. He got up rapture and enthusiasm with an eye on the public" (49). Byron was certainly quirky—he hated the sight of a woman eating, and kept peacocks and monkeys as pets (50)—but this was for show, just like the "curl-papers" he used at night to keep his hair looking, well, Byronic (51). He was notoriously vain, "an absolute egotist" who "courted publicity" (52), all of which suggests shrewd and careful image manipulation, rather than mental illness.

This is supported by Leslie Marchand's definitive two-volume biography of Byron (1956), where there is no psychiatric labeling at all. Instead, Marchand notes that "the seeming contradictions in his nature" reflect his ability to strike "the human balance between idealistic aspiration and realistic disillusionment," and help give him his "refreshing spirit" (53).

Today Byron is most famous for creating (and merging with) the fictional "Byronic" character: the superior, isolated outsider who is always good for some dramatic display or other—in other words, the consummate Romantic hero. In his long poems like "Childe Harold," Byron exalts the handsome scoundrel who is born of nobility, but contemptuous of rank; the scandalous heartthrob who's promiscuous, lives in exile and in debt, and has a dark, mysterious secret (think bodice-ripper novel, with Fabio on the cover). The Byronic hero was certainly larger than life, but he wasn't mentally disordered until psychologists decided to make him so.

For instance, the "mad" Byron got a big plug from Phyllis Grosskurth, a "master of psychoanalytic biography," at least according to her book jacket. In *Byron, the Flawed Angel* (1997), she praises Jamison's "brilliant case" for bipolarity, rather than schizophrenia, and proceeds to tack the loaded modifier "manic" onto a wide variety of his activities, especially the joyful ones. When Byron falls in love, "he was in that manic state when he wanted to proclaim his love from the rooftops" (unlike any "normal" people when they're newly in love).

When he completes a difficult four-mile swim despite strong undercurrents and his club foot, normal triumph is denied him. "Byron's mood had never been so manic," Grosskurth claims, reporting that when he wrote to his friends over the next two months, "his letters were filled with descriptions of the exploit" (54). Clearly, the man was pathological.

Beethoven's Scowl

Such selective reporting occurs with musicians as well as poets, and here Beethoven is a favorite target. Mad genius acolytes often take their "evidence" of mental disorder from one section of the "Heiligenstadt Testament," a will he wrote when he was thirty-two:

> Only art held me back, it seemed impossible to leave the world before I had brought forth all that I felt destined to bring forth, and so I muddled on with this wretched life. (55)

The eminent sanity of the rest of the document is usually ignored:

> O ye men who consider or declare me hostile, obstinate or misanthropic, how greatly you wrong me, you do not know the secret cause of what seems thus to you. My heart and my soul, from childhood on, were filled with tender feelings of good will . . . but just consider that for six years I have been afflicted with an incurable condition, made worse by incompetent physicians . . . born with an ardent, lively temperament . . . I was, at an early age, obliged to cut myself off . . . forgive me if you see me draw back from you, when I would gladly join together with you. (56)

In order to portray Beethoven as the prototypical "mad genius," we must dismiss his deafness and poverty, his serial romantic failures, his ward's suicide attempt, and any other external stressors in favor of some internal maelstrom. This notion gets visual support from that famous scowling image that supposedly came from Beethoven's death mask and became the eternal emblem of his suffering.

In fact, this image was made in 1812 on a living genius who still had fifteen years to go. A tedious and very unpleasant process, it required Beethoven to recline backward thirty-five degrees and get slathered from brow to chin with cold, gooey gypsum. Breathing through quills stuck up his nostrils, he was not allowed to move until the plaster had dried:

> The result exactly replicates not only Beethoven's living face . . . but also his acute physical discomfort—for *this* is what the contracted brow and firmly clamped "scowling" mouth register. **Not a metaphysician's melancholy of soul, but simply the claustrophobic apprehension of near suffocation.** (57, emphasis mine)

Beethoven's pout was also exacerbated by his "double protrusion," a dental condition in which the lips and jaws push forward. But despite any such natural explanations, his suffering face is so symbolic of the tortured genius that it was widely reproduced, both then and now. Today, this miserable image is all most people know of Beethoven.

For my money, history should focus on Beethoven's courage and the enduring beauty he gave us, despite some really bad throws of the cosmic dice. But the myth requires us to focus on his alleged pathology instead. So as long as this area remains resistant to serious research, Beethoven's misery—and the dark suffering expected of all great creatives—will be safe from the clear light of science.

Just two more things before we go. One: I think there's something profoundly mean-spirited about this dogged, postmortem quest to stigmatize people who bring such pleasure to the world. Since the shaky methodology produces nothing useful for science and little that enhances our appreciation of art, why do it?

Two: Perhaps the answer is closer than we think. It might be in the words of writer Tim O'Brien, who said, "As artists, we know the world will break our hearts, but we go on anyway" (58). At last we have it: irrefutable proof of creative madness!

PART FOUR

Eternal Flames

SEVEN

Awesome Powers

The creative person, the person who moves from an irrational source of power, has to face the fact that this
power antagonizes. Under all the superficial praise of the
creative is the desire to kill. It is the old war between the
mystic and the nonmystic, a war to the death.

$\sim$ *May Sarton*

FOR SOME PEOPLE, THIS "OLD WAR" never ends. I once sent Sarton's
words to Stephen Sondheim, who said they were "a source of great
comfort" (1). It surprised me that this incomparable genius needed
any comfort after so many decades of success. It also reminded me of
the us-versus-them dynamic that has kept the mad genius afloat for
over two thousand years.

There are many undercurrents working at it, and, as shown in the
last two chapters, science isn't one of them. But here's the irony, the
paradox, and the rub: in the end it doesn't matter whether the creativity
and madness link is ever proven or not, because the mad genius satis-
fies far too many needs to ever go away. Here's how that works—once
more, even when the examples are musical, the principles are general.

The Stealthy Mood-Shifter

MANY PEOPLE PREFER to get their high-wire thrills vicariously, tingling
from the safety of their seats. They would rather watch others take

the big risks, whether it's chasing down a tornado or its psychological equivalent: plunging deep into the murky unconscious and inviting it out to play. Some are so reluctant to let go that they cannot achieve a sense of abandon without artificial assistance—for them, unleashing the id without a chemical excuse seems too much like madness. The genius volunteers to brave the murky unconscious; after unleashing whatever waits there, he even reports back to the rest of us.

Because art can handle chaos, it also has the power to restore control to a fragmented mind. After months of depression, writer William Styron had decided to commit suicide when the sound of Brahms's "Alto Rhapsody" suddenly jarred him out of his despair and made him realize he needed serious help (in this case, hospitalization). Styron's memoir describes how music had reached him when nothing else could, including the people he loved the most (2).

Music's mood-changing capacity seems to be its most popular use. When psychologist John Sloboda asked sixty-seven "regular listeners" what they sought in music, the most common response was "change agent"—a source of relaxation, inspiration, and healing. One person said it made him feel "understood and comforted in pain, sorrow, and bewilderment." Others noted that music helped them connect to emotions they were too busy to notice, as in "music helps me discover what I am actually feeling" (3). This is a formidable function—much faster and cheaper than therapy—but like most aspects of music, people take it for granted unless somebody writes about it.

Robert Burton explained it well four hundred years ago:

[Music] doth extenuate fears and furies, appeaseth cruelty, abateth heaviness . . . and causeth quiet rest; it takes away spleen and hatred . . . It cures all irksomeness and heaviness of the soul. It is a sovereign remedy against despairs and melancholy, and will drive away the devil himself. (4)

Whether music serves to open or close Pandora's box, its extraordinary effects have long been known—making those who control it seem especially powerful. After all, the Greek god Apollo was in charge of music as well as prophecy, and it's no surprise that the first reported poltergeist was a "demon drummer" (5). In mythology, the glorious music of Orpheus so impressed the gods that they let him retrieve his beloved Eurydice from death. Unfortunately, she made the same mistake as Lot's wife when fleeing the destruction of Sodom and Gomorrah—they both turned around for a last look (I always wondered whether that was a transcultural slap at female curiosity and independence. But I digress.)

It's true that music is the invisible art, with the ability to crystallize time (6). It is also uniquely portable. There's even experimental evidence that it truly is "the universal language" everyone says it is. Scientist Manfred Clynes found empirical support for his theory of "essentic forms"—common brain patterns for emotions that are shared by everyone, regardless of country, culture, or level of sophistication.

Clynes asked Australian university students to convey feelings of anger, hate, grief, joy, and reverence by touching a surface that precisely measured their finger pressure. The amplitude and frequency of their emotional expression created distinctive dynamic shapes that were computer-converted into sound waves, and then played for aborigines in central Australia.

Despite living in a settlement so remote that it took eight days to reach it from the nearest town, the bushmen successfully identified the emotional sound shapes of the white urban students, particularly anger, grief, and joy (7). Similar results were obtained in Mexico, Japan, and Bali. The ancient theory about "music of the spheres" also links it to the cosmic harmonies of pure mathematics and astrology. As far as I can see, music's only limitation is that the word itself, which comes straight from the Greek "moo-si-KEE," has no equivalent synonym, forcing me to be continually redundant as I write about it. But that's a small price to pay.

Body Talk

THERE'S NO DOUBT that music is everywhere. No matter how often it's trivialized in elevators and supermarkets, it's also woven deeper into the social fabric than any other creative endeavor. There are no ballets in airport lounges and no films to watch on the supermarket express line, but there is music coming from every side and for every purpose, whether privately delivered through ear buds or publicly blared in a shopping mall.

Without words, music is as ambiguous as a Rorschach test. As such, it requires listeners to use their own psychology to make meaning of it—to invest mental effort, to lean in and meet it halfway—which deepens its incursion into the psyche. Not all music requires the same effort, of course; sonic wallpaper makes no demands on its listeners, and hardly a dent in their perceptions.

But there are always involuntary factors at work beneath awareness. Unlike other types of creative expression, music has well-documented connections to body and brain—it rides in on sound waves that, when channeled through an ultrasonic scalpel at 23,000 cycles per second, are strong and subtle enough to liquefy tumors. The right frequencies can also cut through steel.

Direct brain measures show that music activates the same pleasure systems that respond to food, sex, and recreational drugs, while recent research demonstrates that playing jazz with others—specifically in that rapid, call-and-response format called "trading fours"—activates the same neural circuitry behind emotional expressiveness in language (8).

People have marveled at music's subliminal effects for centuries. In his 1702 "Essay of Musick," British theater critic Jeremy Collier asked,

> What can be more strange, than that the rubbing of a little hair and catgut together, should make such a mighty alteration in a man that sits at a distance? (9)

That's still a good question. We do know that music affects pulse, breathing, and the skin's responsiveness to electricity (a measure of arousal). It also impacts levels of stress, endurance, and the sensation of tension and release—and it can do all this with a song fragment floating by on the wind.

Music can trigger memories, no matter how old and deeply buried. It can also short-circuit normal physiological reactions; for example, it helps create ritual trances where people stab themselves without bleeding and dance into fire without pain (10). But enumerating all of its effects still can't explain its power to quiet our chattering preoccupations, and take our deepest feelings out for a walk.

We also don't know what draws people to one piece rather than another. Simonton once gathered up 1,919 works by 172 classical composers written at the end of their lives. These "swan songs," while shorter and less original than other pieces (again, as rated by computer), were more popular with the public and also judged more "profound" by musicologists (11). Perhaps people were responding to a subtle distillation of sadness, like Clynes's universal "grief forms."

Music can also ambush the toughest guy. In the history of American film, there are few heroes more admired than Humphrey Bogart's Rick Blaine, in *Casablanca*. Although his past is kept ambiguous, we know it was full of serious dangers, and that Rick conquered them all—all, that is, except for a song. In his "gin joint," he strictly forbids the playing of "As Time Goes By," the theme of his lost love, for fear he'll be undone by what it stirs up. But Sam plays it again, and for that moment he has more power to hurt Rick than any Nazi attack.

Since music can calm things down as well as stir them up, it is regularly used for healing. During the Renaissance, it was even said to cure the bubonic plague (12). Neurologist Oliver Sacks, in his *Awakenings* (both the 1973 book and 1990 movie), describes how people who can't talk or move can dance, while music therapists continue to work daily miracles with all kinds of difficulty and pain.

Finally, music also makes a reliable training tool, not only when played as a reward, but when interrupted or removed to send the opposite message (13). It's conceivable that an incessant desire for music could be considered an addiction, given how its absence can cause so much stress (ever take ear buds and an iPod away from a teenager?). For all we know, "music addiction" might pop up in the next DSM, complete with the usual pharmaceutical fixes waiting in the wings.

Musician = Magician

IT's FITTING THAT these words are just two letters apart, since the efforts of musicians can affect every living thing, from surface to core. And the great ones, the Big C's of music, are off the chart altogether. I'm not alone in thinking they tap a deeper mystery than other artists. Even legendary film director Ingmar Bergman compares them to prophets and saints, since they all "touch the ineffable" (14).

The downside of musicians' ability to create with something others cannot see, understand, or manipulate is that it emphasizes their "otherness," which is the outer ring of madness. This is how the mad genius gets to be both mighty creator and evil magician at the same time:

> In the myth itself one can discern the feeling of ambivalence that has always accompanied the great of this world . . . this dual characterization of the artist, at once both admirable and dangerous, regularly reappears in traditional accounts and persists in actively shaping the attitudes of his contemporaries to him. (15)

Their sorcery enables them to wrestle their troubles to the mat, and neutralize their heartache; as pianist Karl Schnabel explains,

> Musicians can dare to handle emotions that would kill any other human being. If your love isn't reciprocated, you may stand at the window 30 floors up and want to jump. Instead, we jump to the keyboard. Then the emotion is used; it's not dangerous anymore. (16)

Of course, other artists transmute suffering into beauty, but no one else offers a solution you can hum. Ideally, musicians' efforts will lead them to flow, when the barriers between the self and musical expression seem to disappear. As pianist and educator Shelly Berg put it, "When I play, the piano disappears—it's not an instrument, it's an amplifier" (17). This echoes the Chinese concept of "artistic ecstasy," where creation becomes part of the creator (18). The ultimate musical joy is when the band and the audience are all sharing the flow together.

The problem is that this event—Monty Alexander's "moment"— is as unpredictable as a drop-in from the Muse. But this keeps musicians in the game for the same reason the gambler keeps betting: every once in a while, they both win. Alexander describes the magic when

> every living thing within the radius is reacting. Even the cock-roach coming out of the wall is going . . . yeah! It's a wave, it's a power. It happens at that indefinable moment that nothing can force, and once again, it's time to get out of the way. (19)

This glorious feeling can be achieved in other creative arenas as well. I once got "in the zone" by playing tennis, when I suddenly aced every shot, knew precisely where and when to run, and sent my opponents scrambling all over the court. At the end, I could even leap over the net without catching my heel and falling on my face. It was absolutely wondrous—and it never happened again.

Genius Envy

ASIDE FROM THEIR special powers, there are more worldly reasons to envy the highly talented who devote themselves to art. One is that creative lives seem to have more passion than most. While it's always better for people to enjoy their work, the notion of having to "love" it seems rather immature—after all, society depends on people doing their jobs whether they love them or not.

Many great creatives feel such a deep calling to their art that they never consider any other life. This kind of devotion, especially in the face of such dubious rewards, is more characteristic of religious vocations. Both paths provide a clarity of purpose that most people never achieve.

Another benefit is the lack of helicopter bosses; studies suggest that creativity is actually undermined by direct surveillance (20). Then there's the freedom to stay up and sleep late, a luxury usually associated with vacation, adolescence, and New Year's Eve. But these advantages are trivial compared to the possibility that creatives might leave their footprints in the sand—that their art may be important or beautiful enough to outlive them. None of this endears them to the hardworking discontented.

Nor does the fact that although most creatives work very hard, much of it is private; this can make them seem lazy and self-indulgent, particularly to those who have less respect for internal accomplishments. There's also that irritating refusal to surrender their dreams to a paycheck—to many, this is sufficient proof of craziness, all by itself.

It's true that creatives who work at home don't have to find a clean shirt or a parking space, or smile at people they despise, and their schedule is largely under their own control. Yet this freedom comes with a hidden price—those same freelancers, so content in their sweats and long private days, may be anguishing over making their rent. But musicians don't really work—they "play." Right?

It does seem that way, especially when they seem to get more sexual attention than other people. At parties, musicians provide a warm hearth for people to gather around; onstage, a great, passionate musician sends out sparks that few other creatives can match (authors reading their books are rarely pelted with panties). Then there's the unique phenomenon of "plaster casters"—female music fans who create replicas of male genitalia they have known, and display them like the hunters' trophies they are. Some people even find music more exciting than sex. Out of 249 people who participated in a study about thrills, 96 percent cited music as their top tingle, with sex lagging far behind at 70 percent (21).

Musicians have had groupies ever since Apollo strummed his first lyre. In the 1800s, composer Jacques Offenbach was so adored that society ladies in Boston unhitched his horses and pulled his carriage through the streets themselves. In 1985, when the band Dire Straits sang about "money for nothing and your chicks for free," they were satirizing people's fantasies about the easy lives and conquests of musicians.

Even if the sexual advantage is more imagined than real, there's always a little green-eyed monster padding behind any genius. New research suggests that envy actually comes in two varieties: benign and malicious. Both compensate the envier for any painful inequities in position, but they have completely opposite effects. The first is productive, since it motivates people to achieve more success for themselves and thus close the gap between themselves and the envied person. The second is destructive, because it only inspires people to tear that person down.

The whole thing hinges on deservingness: the judgment that a fortunate person is worthy of his advantage because he earned it (benign), or he doesn't deserve it because it came from luck (malicious). Malicious envy can be so vicious that some high achievers are especially nice to potential enviers, much like the nervous puppy who rolls over and shows her belly to an aggressor, as if to say "I'm not a threat!" (22). After all, we wouldn't need a cliché like "don't hide your light under a bushel" if it weren't so common for exceptional talents to downplay their gifts. Modesty is only part of the reason—the rest is defensive.

Fortunately, creative freedom may even include immunity to the myth. In 2002 my survey of top jazz musicians showed that far from being hurt or hobbled by the mad genius label, these supremely talented people were too busy making music to care (23). This was no surprise, since opting for a jazz career is already a sign of independence from public approval. Composer Clare Fischer put it particularly well:

In my case as a composer, I am not interested in what perception is, but what my feelings are when I write. This does not make me follow what is current, but leaves me in my own world. In relationship to sane or insane—I might add that there are many who find me strange, opinionated (that means I believe something) and as such I answer them by saying, "Had they known my mother, they would see what a beautiful job I've done with what I was given." (24)

A final advantage of the musical life is its unending challenge. The complexities of jazz can keep its players stimulated and busy for a lifetime; musical activity may even postpone the cognitive effects of aging (25). After a 1986 concert, I witnessed this exchange:

> Delighted fan, gushing: "You still got it, Diz."
> Dizzy Gillespie, grinning: "I'm still seekin' it!"

This helps explain all those elderly greats who keep playing until they die, or very close to it. Jazz is also a profession that actually reveres—and even employs —its elder statesmen. But here comes the mad genius myth to neutralize any sting: "By salting their exalted position with stigma, we somehow reduce them so that petty people like us can more comfortably accept their existence" (26). Condescension is a big comfort too:

> An artist who is widely admired may be worthy of consideration if he or she has suffered a miserable life. This gets a lot of drunks and junkies into the Pantheon on a pass. There is an implicit condescension in this process: I can admire him because I feel sorry for him, affirming my own superiority. Condescension to brilliance is the ultimate arrogance. (27)

Such haughtiness can mute some of the resentment, but can never eliminate it. This furious and pained description of creative persecution comes from psychologist Eysenck, in his autobiography, *Rebel with a Cause* (1997):

> After reading book after book about creative people one thing stood out above all others, and that was the hostile, malevolent, rancorous, vicious, fiendish, savage, malicious, defamatory, slanderous, spiteful, venomous, and vindictive attitude of the mediocre orthodoxy towards anything novel, original, creative, fresh, ingenious, innovative, seminal, unusual or nonconformist. (28)

Genius envy is a long-running melody that shows no signs of ever fading away.

Shrinks Are People Too

MENTAL HEALTH PROFESSIONALS are not exempt from any of this. First of all, they work in a field that has never been known for its exuberance. In fact, many therapists see their job as reining in human wildness—keeping the lid on the id.

It doesn't help that psychological and artistic viewpoints are inherently opposed. For example, artists harbor "the attitude of abandon in which [the artist] feels his inspiration and allows it to develop . . . without regard for rule, meaning, or the technique of analysis." This is the exact opposite of the scientific approach.

All of this can create jealousy of lives that seem freer and more passionate than their own. There will always be those who retaliate with the sharpest weapon they have: a psychiatric label that diminishes both those enviable people and whatever they may create. This is a tactic as old as psychology itself: "Freud's condescending attitude and outright hostility toward great artists is evident in all his writings. He makes a problem out of art," says Szasz (29).

Freud's not alone, either. Therapists who believe that all creatives harbor mental disorders are more likely to be patronizing, focusing on their clients' supposed "illness" than their strengths.

It's also common for people to resent those who baffle them and make them feel inferior. One solution is to push the offenders down and away by equating their special talents with disability. Psychologists can accomplish this with a focus on "psychoticism." This is a personality construct developed by Eysenck to describe the cognitive tendency toward "overinclusiveness," or "admitting unusual associations and ideas" (30).

When psychoticism spins out of control, a person's thoughts snap free of their moorings and fly off into wild schizophrenic nonsense. But people with strong egos are safe: they can harness this loose and expansive thinking to power their creative flights without ever losing contact with the ground.

Unfortunately, the word itself includes insanity. Even if Eysenck frames it as conducive to genius and creativity (31), it's literally so close to "psychotic" that it can only reinforce the perception that creative equals crazy. It doesn't help that society already expects the arts to be the refuge of misfits.

Group Sax

Music has both a positive and negative impact on groups: it facilitates bonding between people, but can also be used for punishment and control. First: if there's any doubt that music has the power to connect large groups of people, just attend any ethnic wedding or outdoor concert, whether it's Justin Bieber or Jimmy Buffett.

Music also marks common life passages, freezing special moments for all eternity: a hit summer love song can evoke an old affair in vivid detail, down to the feel of sand in your bathing suit. That's why late-night TV is forever peddling historic compilations, while ghost groups (big bands, Motown) roam the countryside, inviting people to relive the '40s or '50s or '60s when they probably had more hope, and certainly more hair. Music serves as the bridge between their personal and group identities.

The Romans were so wary of the bonding powers of music that

they banned instruments, hoping to keep their conquered populations from using them to gather and unify. A similar rationale supposedly motivated plantation owners to keep drums away from their African slaves—they were threatened by the possibility of transmitting secret messages as well as the communal force of the gathering itself. I once heard that resourceful slaves invented tap dancing to replace the drum messages, but I have no way of verifying that one.

Other music that is deliberately used to pump up energy and cohesiveness includes national anthems, work songs, and war chants. Bonding also occurs with hymns, story-songs and folk ballads, all of which help convey and preserve a community's values from one generation to another.

Finally, much of the world's most emotionally powerful music was first created by oppressed minorities to assert their pride and solidarity. For example, in America, we have the blues; in Greece, there's bouzouki; in Portugal, fado; and in Spain, flamenco. There's also reggae and similar "roots" music wherever people need to have it. This raw, deeply felt music is inevitably adopted by the larger culture, becoming a source of national satisfaction and making serious money, but rarely for its originators.

Music also leaps over political boundaries, enabling the people behind them to connect with each other. Years ago, in another incarnation, I took the captain of a Russian oil tanker out to lunch. At first this was awkward since he spoke little English and the only Russian I knew were the names of composers and vodkas. But over the soup course we found a musical bridge, and somehow ended up singing a Yiddish song that we both learned as children. It was a warm moment between strangers who shared no other language.

Music as Manipulation

MUSIC IS CONSIDERABLY less endearing when used for manipulation. One possible exception is Muzak, the pop music that is programmed in fifteen-minute segments of ascending tempo and brassiness to propel office workers through their day, especially over those mid-afternoon energy slumps. Peppy as it is, even Muzak is a form of subliminal control.

There's a long history of regulating music for social purposes, whether it was considered too potent in itself, or just something people wanted that could be taken away. In ancient China, each emperor had a Bureau of Music to establish standards for pitch, much like the modern regulation of weights and measures. They believed that deviations from the norm could be troublesome; so did Plato, who warned that music had to be kept simple and predictable, or it would threaten the state (32).

About two millennia later, Charles IX of France put it this way:

> It is of great importance for the morals of the citizens of a town that the music current in the country should be kept under certain laws . . . whenever music is disordered, morals are also depraved. (33)

This suspicion was shared by the Nazis, who prohibited jazz, including the use of the dreaded "wah-wah mute." Stalin banned it too, along with any other music that was considered too challenging or individualistic. Western sounds were verboten during the Chinese cultural revolution of the '60s, and in 1979 the Ayatollah stripped all the music from Iranian radio and television because it was "too much like opium . . . stupefying persons listening to it and making their brains inactive and frivolous."

This resembles some of the speeches in the 1984 film *Footloose*, in which music and dancing were suppressed to protect the morality of teenagers. At least it had a happy ending, as compared to the Taliban who punish musicians caught in the act by beating them with their own instruments and throwing them in jail (34). And then there's jazz, which is supposedly particularly dangerous to virgins—at least it was in 1922:

> Moral disaster is coming to hundreds of young American girls

through the pathological, nerve-irritating, sex-exciting music of jazz orchestras, according to the Illinois Vigilance Association. In Chicago alone the association's representatives have traced the fall of 1,000 girls in the last two years to jazz music. (35)

Aside from corrupting people, music also has the power to punish them. In April of 2000, college students who hid beer in their dorms were supposedly "punished" by having to attend a performance of the opera *Tosca* (36). In malls, stores play "easy listening" music to keep teenagers from lurking too close. In 1993, U.S. government agents encouraged cult members in Waco, Texas, to end their siege by assaulting them with endless choruses of "These Boots Are Made for Walking."

This was not the first time Americans used music as a weapon. In 1989, U.S. troops pelted fugitive dictator Manuel Noriega with fifteen days of hard rock, and during the Persian Gulf War, they blasted heavy metal into Kuwait. More recently, Iraqi detainees have reportedly endured super-loud repetitions of "I Love You" by Barney the Dinosaur, along with what many consider the ultimate torture: the jingle for Meow Mix.

At Least It's Not Contagious

I BELIEVE MENTAL health is a continuum we all share, with the most serious problems isolated to one end or the other and most people wandering safely between them. Others would rather isolate the allegedly disordered to another track altogether, making them qualitatively different from everyone else. This is yet another reason to preserve the mad genius myth: it helps thicken the wall between us and them.

In my seventeen years of teaching psychology, most of my students hated the idea of sharing a sanity spectrum with the disturbed, even if the undesirables were clearly huddled far away, at the extreme end. The chance of finding some commonality was just too frightening. Psychologist John Rhead writes about what happens when we encounter madness in others:

One can hardly be such an observer for very long without no-
ticing, perhaps ever so slightly, one's own capacity for madness.
The anxiety stirred by such awareness, especially when it is not
fully conscious, seems to me to be a factor in all the brutality,
both historic and modern, directed at those who are experiencing psychosis. (37)

It's true that there's always been hostility in the mad genius myth—
as Sarton said, it's the old war between the mystic and the non-mystic,
a war to the death. So long as those Big C's are kept strictly separate—
genetically blighted is best—it keeps us safe from whatever "they"
have. It also levels the playing field, since if we can't have the abilities
of genius, at least we won't have to share their suffering. In any case,
it's always better to focus on artistic anguish—whether real or imagined—than on painful disparities in talent.

This helps explain society's frequent resentment toward its most
creative members. Since nobody knows why some folks are especially
gifted and others are not, and the myth says nothing about geniuses
doing any hard work, it's easy to perceive them as being mysteriously—and thus unfairly—blessed. And so their awesome, irrational
powers, together with their supposed lack of "deservingness," combine
to ignite the malice that simmers just beneath that pejorative psychiatric labeling. This also feeds the widespread fascination with creative
downfalls and disasters.

Luckily, regardless of what the public hopes and expects, the Big
C's of the world will keep breaking ground where others have never
been, bringing back treasures no one ever imagined, and creating new
beauty that lifts the heart. But as long as they dare to exercise those
singular and awesome powers—whether their tool is a piano or a
paintbrush—they will continue to be ripe for myth making, including
the ones that incubate in resentment and make madmen of them all.

EIGHT

They Must Be Crazy

The music business is a cruel and shallow money trench,
a long plastic hallway where thieves and pimps run free,
and good men die like dogs. There's also a negative side.
~ *Hunter S. Thompson*

WHEN YOU GATHER IT ALL together, it's easy to see why our geniuses are expected to be mad. Who else would tolerate such a long and lonely struggle for the sake of such unpredictable and relatively transient satisfaction? They *must* be crazy, right?

Even if science manages to verify or destroy the myth, other things will keep it going forever. The daunting reality of many creative lives tends to provoke questions like, "Do you have to be crazy to be a professional musician [painter, poet, dancer], or does it just help?" and "Do you actually make a living doing that?" Another theory holds that the artistic life can make anyone crazy, even those who were perfectly sane to begin with. No one moves in a vacuum, not even the exceptional minds who seem so above it all.

But whether you believe this career attracts or creates craziness—or even both—there's no arguing that it's a particularly difficult one, fraught with vocational hazards that could create a mad genius all by themselves.

Welcome to the Stresstival

THE OLD PICTURE of creatives as isolated bubble-dwellers has been curling up at the edges and joined by a new focus on training, opportunity, stress, encouragement, colleagues, and icons. Some are finally recognizing that artistic mood simply depends on how well the work is going at any given moment.

There's no guarantee that the most talented will receive their just recognition and reward, any more than life promises fairness in general. But the musical world—and the jazz path in particular—have some extra challenges to stumble over. These include the ongoing discrepancy between the value of your work and what the public will pay; the difficulty of determining and communicating that value (and often, believing in it); the lack of standards for payment that are both widely accepted and enforceable; the frequent insult of having to wait forever for your pitiful pay; and—increasingly—the risk of someone stealing your product. Given all the rampant piracy today, the only thing musicians can own is their live performance—and even that can go straight to YouTube without their making a penny on the deal. They must be crazy!

Some of this can be traced back to ancient Greece, where it was customary not to pay artists whose creations were divinely inspired. This set an unfortunate precedent: "Even in our own days, society still retains the belief that renunciation and poverty are the lot of the genius" (1). All freelancers face financial risk, but musicians often get paid badly because people think they will do the work for the sake of exposure or publicity (and many do). In 2002, 66 percent of jazz musicians in San Francisco earned less than $7,000, even those with postcollege education (2). Saxophonist-author Greg Fishman explains the dilemma of choosing whether to make money or art:

> The creative process is like a thirst that has to be quenched. The price we pay for this enjoyment is quite high . . . it's our love for the music that allows us to be exploited in many cases. I could

go on to get a doctorate, sign a record deal, and the local club still pays the same $90 a night that it did 15 years ago. I suppose the smart thing to do, financially, is to take a high paying job supplying musical wallpaper to the corporate world, or background music for a wedding, but my music is too important to me for that. You start to make compromises in the art when you get hired to perform "functional" music . . . where you're a name in a checklist, along with the rented tablecloths and the centerpieces. (3)

Advances in technology have made it possible for anyone to make a CD. Although many indie records are terrific, this has contributed to record labels disappearing, collapsing into one another, or being acquired by giant corporations that have little interest or experience in music. This has created a perfect storm of public confusion. In the past, when musicians grumbled about who got deals and who didn't, there were gatekeepers to provide some illusion of quality control, even if they caught their share of suspicion and resentment.

Now there's no one to funnel the flood and help separate lasting excellence from something that rises to brief success on a twittering wave (there will always be critics, but they have their own credibility problems, as we will see). This makes it even harder for musicians to sustain their motivation. So does the perception that they're only as good as their last gig, which generates additional pressure; this problem is shared by other creatives as well.

A stressor more specific to music is being treated like hired help, rather than artists. Virtually every performer has a war story that illustrates the genius's paradox of being admired and demeaned at the same time. Here's one of the best, from guitarist Wayne Wright:

I was about to walk on to do my show one night when a man in the audience stopped me and said, "Wayne, do me a favor before you go on. Could I have your autograph . . . and some more butter?" (4)

Such tales could easily fill another book, but for now I'll just share a list of gig stressors that guitarist Tuck Andress, of the duo of Tuck and Patti, sent into cyberspace some years ago:

Locked bathroom and way too many liquids before long show; drunks falling onstage, drunks disrobing on stage; bass player playing random notes and rhythms because he is not a bass player at all but nonetheless booked the gig; drummer watching ball game on portable TV with headphones throughout performance or drummer announcing that he killed somebody just before the show.

Sometimes musicians trip over the tangle of definitions the experts have put in their way, such as, if creativity cannot be separated from its recognition, how can a player be creative if nobody hears what he's playing? Like any other Stresstival challenge, fighting this one requires building strong self-esteem and then keeping it alive.

It doesn't help when the same invisibility that intensifies music's impact makes it harder to hold on to successes—if you didn't record what you just played, was it really as good as you thought it was? Yes? Well, after the last notes vanish and the applause fades away, where's the evidence?

The chronic inconsistency of performance is another familiar and mysterious hazard. You may be just as trained, talented, psyched, and prepared as ever, but one night you can do nothing wrong; and the next, nothing right (others might not notice anything different, which evokes yet another trap: the tyranny of creative perfectionism).

The problem could be that pre-performance taco, an unresponsive or noisy audience, or the bad news that came in your last phone call. Such capriciousness can madden any creative, but musicians are particularly vulnerable because they essentially *are* what they *play*:

For reasons that go beyond the finality of each performance, the performing arts actually challenge the artist's equilibrium with regard to self-esteem more severely than do other creative activities . . . [he] is likely to be more profoundly affected by his reception than a creator who has fashioned a thing or a concept separate from the physical self. (5)

Being on the road is also punishing, given the strains of sleep deprivation and constant adjustment to alien food, quarters, language, and climate. The vocal group New York Voices once traveled for twenty-eight straight hours to play in Japan for thirty minutes. Ironically, another stressor can arrive after an especially successful engagement; as jazz violinist Graham Clark describes it,

> There's a particularly desolate feeling I sometime get if I have played in a well-filled venue. You finish the set, do the encore, go backstage, have a beer, and when you go back out, the hall is empty. Where a few minutes before, there were several hundred people having a great time, there is now a cold emptiness . . . that is something that most people don't understand. Surely you must feel great after a really packed gig? Well, while you are playing you do, but there can be a terrible anti-climax. (6)

Traveling can also wreak havoc with relationships. Given that half of all marriages end in divorce, this danger is hardly restricted to musicians. But it doesn't help when spouses are distant—out on the road or deep in their own heads during hours of solo practicing—or when any romantic or family plan can be trumped by the unexpected gig that must be accepted to stay in the game. Relationship stress is compounded when the best opportunities for intimate healing are blocked—when couples climb into bed on completely different schedules or on completely different continents.

Playing music can have serious physical consequences as well. Musicians can easily hurt themselves in the intensity of practice or performance. Carpal tunnel syndrome and other repetitive stress injuries are common. Vocalists are additionally prone to "Las Vegas voice," or strained vocal cords from working smoky rooms (fortunately, this may be decreasing, as fewer people are willing to mortgage their homes for a carton of cigarettes).

And since health insurance is a rarity, a serious illness or injury can derail a career; for instance, a trumpet player with dental problems can lose it all (Freddie Hubbard, Buck Clayton). When a ballplayer has to quit, he opens a string of car washes—the musician, on the other hand, is more likely to wind up in a job that requires a paper hat.

Critical Conditions

WHAT OTHER BUSINESS comes with a trailing horde that judges everything you do, and then shares this verdict in an authoritative public forum? Politics and sports come to mind, both of which tend to pay a bit better than music. Critics have been a major stressor ever since Aristotle first tagged musicians as "vulgar," and sniffed that "it is not manly to perform music except when drunk or for fun" (7).

Even the greatest musicians who ever lived had their share of grief from critics. Beethoven was severely chastised in his day for his "too-exuberant conceptions"; since he broke away from the classical tradition of Mozart and Haydn, his work was "totally misunderstood by the general public." One critic viciously described his second symphony as "a filthy monster, a wounded dragon writhing hideously, refusing to die" (8).

At least he was in good company. Although Bach was popular as an organist and conductor, he was undervalued as a composer: "never understood, let alone recognized, during his lifetime" (9). Now Tchaikowsky is a giant, but in 1881 his violin concerto "pose[d] for the first time the appalling notion that there can be works of music that stink to the ear" (10). Georges Bizet, composer of the beloved opera *Carmen*, died three months after its premiere—he only saw the public's apathy, and never knew his enormous success. It's no wonder he is quoted as saying, "Music: what a splendid art, but what a wretched profession!"

Closer to our own time, composer-conductor Leonard Bernstein dismissed the great George Gershwin as a mere "melodist":

The Rhapsody [in Blue] is not a composition at all. It's a string of separate paragraphs stuck together with a thin paste of flour and water. Composing is a very different thing from writing tunes. (11)

Given the snarky tone of that comment, it sounds like Bernstein was jealous of Gershwin's popularity. There are also critics who envy those who do what they can only write about—Mel Brooks once said they "can't even make music by rubbing their back legs together." Again, Monty Alexander said it best:

You have to be made of steel. You have to affirm, reaffirm things that you know are good and true and right, and you eventually wake up one day and say—man, you can't do what I can do, which is just to sit there and close your eyes and this music stuff comes out. (12)

It's always possible to defuse a nasty review by blaming the ignorance, attitude, or lack of "ears" of the person who wrote it. But it's not easy to ignore the impact of bad press on one's ability to make a living. Critical rejection also makes it harder to keep self-doubt at bay, especially given the unrelenting drive to perform consistently at high levels (13). As Shelly Berg explains,

Why is it healthy or desirable to dress down a well-intentioned artist in a public forum? Artist egos are very fragile, regardless of the personae they radiate. It hurts and can be very damaging to have someone write that you suck. Most often, the negative comments are the result of a subjective, style-based judgment from the bias of the critic, as opposed to whether or not the artist achieved what he/she was intending. (14)

In order to face all the inherent risks of this career, the musician must be a person of courage—a necessity that was evident two thousand years ago, when

> the Roman poet Horace . . . noted that it is both essential and supremely difficult to maintain one's own standards in the face of popular disaffection . . . Indeed, it does take valor to be a performing artist. (15)

The Bohemian Excuse

THE FLIP SIDE to being victimized by the myth is to spread it yourself. Counting on the public belief that its Big C's will behave outrageously, some creatives use their talents—whether actual or alleged—to justify moodiness, irresponsibility, and other forms of self-indulgence. This is the "Bohemian excuse," according to that very sane genius Steve Allen (16), although with typical generosity, he attributed it to his wife, Jayne.

Aside from getting a permanent pass on bad behavior, creative people who impersonate mad geniuses can maintain some consistent identity in a life full of occupational stops and starts ("I might not be gigging right now, but I am a crazy creative—just watch!"). This helps to remind impatient observers that their genius still exists, even if there hasn't been a new book or CD or painting in years. And the artist who views inspiration as heaven-sent—externalized and mystical—can't be blamed for lacking ideas.

There are also career advantages to being outrageous (see, for instance, singer Lady Gaga's meat dress). Sometimes being outrageous is the whole career, as when reality TV "star" Snooki boasts that she wakes up in a garbage can once a month. This brings us back to considering whether some famously bizarre geniuses were truly victims of mental disorder, or simply clever entertainers who acted as though they were.

For example, the peculiar ways of Thelonious Monk have been

variously attributed to schizophrenia, manic depression, and obsessive-compulsive personality disorder—all of which make a symptom out of his quirky, original music. But in the Monk documentary *Straight, No Chaser*, there are clues that he is absolutely in charge—or, as my father used to say, "crazy like a fox."

In the midst of some signature spinning, Monk stops for a brief aside. "It's difficult to decipher," says music professor Gabriel Solis, "but the essence is something like, 'They say I'm crazy, but I know what I'm doing. If you were just anybody and did that they'd lock you up, but I do it and they love it'" (17). His definitive biographer Robin Kelley also quotes him as saying, "Sometimes it's to your advantage for people to think you're crazy" (18).

There are musicians who deliberately imitate their truly troubled icons, hoping to borrow some of their magic. Saxophonist Jackie McLean describes young players who were not drug-addicted, but tried to look like they were: "eyes half-closed, striking their slouched pose, because all the people we admired had fallen prey" (19). Many see Bird's chemical problems as integral to his brilliance. As bassist Dick Egner told me,

> Tortured heroes have some kind of "glamour appeal." In fifteen years on the road, I can remember forgiving hours of musical blathering from drunk or high musicians in the hopes that the moment of transcendence was at hand. (20)

Fellow bass player Chuck Israels complained about the overly permissive attitude towards artists by a public that would find the actions of the people in question inexcusable in other circumstances: "This has sometimes encouraged people with whom I've worked to exaggerate this behavior, sometimes to my considerable chagrin" (21).

For some people, the pose of eccentricity also protects them from the demands of the world. In *The Mad Genius Controversy* (1978), George Becker explains how the Romantic poets of the nineteenth century used their supposed creative madness:

The aura of madness served the function of differentiating genius from the mean, the mediocre, or the bourgeois . . . **the man of genius could claim some of the powers and privileges granted the "fool" [and] the "possessed" prophet.** (22, emphasis mine)

The truth is, it's impossible to know how much intensity is faked just to borrow a little stardust from genius. For example, when a researcher reports that writers are more sensitive to electric shock than other people, is this because they truly *are*, or just more likely to say so, because it feeds the expectation and the fantasy (23)?

Part of the enduring appeal of trumpeter Miles Davis is his brooding image, just as singer Billie Holiday powered her legacy with victimhood. For the record, Holiday wrote neither melody nor lyrics to "Strange Fruit," the profound and heartbreaking song that is often associated with her. Jazz writer Nat Hentoff notes that "Billie's response to racism was considerably more resilient and defiant than is apparent in the soap-opera movie which purports to be about her life" (24).

Gene Lees objects to similar fictions about the tragedy of singer Edith Piaf:

I do not share it. Born literally on a sidewalk from a slut of a mother who had no interest in her, this indestructible child of the streets climbed with cunning and courage to the highest level of the international entertainment world. (25)

But since eventually "a person becomes the thing he is described as being" (26), the truth is easily buried under piles of press clippings. And public expectations about mad geniuses can even encourage their risky behavior:

The American artistic landscape is littered with the corpses of the brilliant, from painter Mark Rothko to poet Anne Sexton to musician Charlie Parker, and one must wonder if they died in part because sycophants with safer lives so celebrated their excesses. (27)

While we're on the subject of cheerleaders, something should be said about enablers. These are the spouses, siblings, parents, and children who permit their creatives to act selfishly and irresponsibly, and who scramble to keep every domestic distraction at bay, because Their Genius Must Always Come First. Since their behavior emphasizes the fragility of the artist, it adds more credence to the myth—but at least it helps to neutralize any resentment at home.

The myth is also very good for selling product. According to historian Alice Echols, who wrote *Scars of Sweet Paradise: The Life and Times of Janis Joplin* (1999),

> Janis Joplin was keenly aware of the public's desire for story after story of her flamboyant exploits and her underlying unhappiness. She even told a reporter for *Rolling Stone* that people like their blues singers miserable. She was very much attached to the idea that her audience was buying a whole package, and she demanded that the press cover it. (28)

Public posturing aside, some notable artists have bought the myth themselves, and genuinely believe that the best music comes from suffering. Singer k. d. lang has said, "I don't think I'd be as good a singer if I didn't have that depth of pain" (29). In a 1998 VH1 special, pop icon Billy Joel claimed that manic depression is "actually helpful" to musicians: "I'm glad Beethoven didn't get psychoanalyzed and take Prozac," he said, "because we would've missed all this wonderful music."

Being "Out" Is Being "In"

CREATIVE PEOPLE THROW more kindling on the mad genius fire each time they emphasize their role as "outsiders." This stance can be so central to their self-image that they often backpedal away when it looks like they're getting some mainstream success: "Whenever they risked becoming members of 'the establishment' they would again shift course to attain at least intellectual marginality" (30).

For good and evil, the marginality of jazz is never in danger, given that it's been six decades since it was considered America's popular music. For years, it has claimed only a tiny sliver of the music market. But this position also provides great cohesion, since few things solidify a group more than being in jeopardy. Each time people join together to prop up a sagging banner, it increases their devotion to the cause. Every cult leader knows this, including Freud, who virtually guaranteed the continuance of psychoanalysis by emphasizing its rejection by the medical mainstream.

In fact, being "out" can be cooler than being "in." Here's what attracted pianist and songwriter Dave Frishberg to jazz musicians:

> These were magic people who could casually play songs in any key, talked passionately about "chord changes," and whose repertoire was seemingly limitless. Jazz musicians were hip, they were funny, they were sensitive, they were clannish, and they always had the best girlfriends. I liked being around jazz players, and I wanted to be one of them. (31)

Years later, Frishberg and Bob Dorough wrote the anthemic "I'm Hip," their fond spoof on the jazz "cat." Here's part of that classic tune:

> I'm too much. I'm a gas.
> I am anything but middle class.
> When I hang around the band,
> Poppin' my thumbs, diggin' the drums,
> Squares don't seem to understand
> Why I flip. They're not hip like I'm hip . . .
> Cuz I'm cool as a cuke.
> I'm a cat, I'm a card, I'm a kook.

I get so much out of life,
Really I do. Skoo ba dee boo.
One more time play "Mack the Knife."
Let 'er rip. I may flip, but I'm hip. (32)

An early study of jazz musicians describes how they choose to bind together with "self-segregating" slang, attitudes, and behavior:

> The musician is conceived of as an artist who possesses a mysterious artistic gift setting him apart from all other people . . . Feeling their difference strongly, musicians like-wise believe they are under no obligation to imitate the conventional behavior of squares . . . accordingly, behavior which flouts conventional social norms is greatly admired [and] is a primary occupational value. (33)

Fame: Fear and Fantasy

SUPERSTITION KEEPS THE myth alive too. Fear and suspicion of greatness goes back to our earliest myths about hubris and trespassing. Adam and Eve lost Paradise for being too arrogant, while the Tower of Babel was destroyed for rising too close to the heavens. When Prometheus steals the secret of fire and gives it to the human race, this is such a disloyal empowerment that he must spend eternity chained to a rock, with a vulture gnawing on his liver. Defiance and ambition also killed Icarus, whose homemade wings melted when he flew too close to the sun.

In the rare instances when a mortal is admitted to the exalted realms, it's probably because some dark Faustian bargain has been struck. This payback idea entered the collective mind as far back as Aristotle, who said that heroes can only triumph until they are defeated by one tragic internal flaw or other. This scenario was later perfected by Shakespeare, who showed how Hamlet, Lear, Othello, and Macbeth were brought down by their indecisiveness, pride, jealousy, and ambition (respectively).

For those who worry about angering the gods, being a genius is always dangerous. When George Bernard Shaw wrote to violinist Jascha Heifetz, he was being funny but also voicing a classic concern:

> My wife and I were overwhelmed by your concert. If you continue to play with such beauty, you will certainly die young. No one can play with such perfection without provoking the jealousy of the gods. I earnestly implore you to play something badly every night before going to bed. (34)

In today's Greece, there's an amulet in every shop window—that cobalt-blue circle with the yellow "eye" in the center is supposed to ward off any divine retaliation toward mortals who are too proud of their successes. In some cultures it's considered so risky to verbalize good fortune out loud that the speaker must immediately knock on wood, spit in the wind, or mutter some ritual incantation.

The irony is that things may go downhill for the musician who finally makes it. Fame may be the ultimate fantasy, but it arrives with its own problems. Music groups often break up under the pressure, as when players who were once easy-going are "pushed to extremes of mood by success and adulation from others, as well as by positive or negative criticism" (35).

Existing jealousies can escalate, particularly when some group members get more attention from others. There may be tussles about songwriting between the band members who write the melodies and those who provide the lyrics. According to Johnny Mercer, one of the greatest wordsmiths of all:

> Music, as they see it, is the important art. Everybody uses words, don't they? It takes more talent to write music, but it takes more courage to write lyrics. (36)

It's impossible to discuss competition and resentment without mentioning one of the arch-enemies of jazz: the rich and famous saxophonist

Kenny G[orelick]. In his entertaining *Bad Music* (2004), trombonist, bandleader, and Columbia University professor Chris Washburne explains how Kenny G has made truckloads of money selling his slick and simple sound, the "smooth jazz" that is often confused with the authentic stuff. Many "real" jazz musicians are mocking of Kenny G and his genre, and resent their financial success, although Washburne fairly points out that we cannot dismiss a music that plays such a large role in millions of lives (37). He has a point, but it's unlikely to blunt much bitterness. Please note: I am deliberately refraining from any Kenny G jokes, but I will say that he's the only saxophone player I've ever seen who can blow and smile broadly at the same time.

Another downside to fame is that it attracts hangers-on who don't really care for the musicians as people, but want to come along for the ride: they are the pilot fish of show business. These hollow connections can compound any isolation and loneliness musicians are already feeling, particularly when the adoration of thousands is followed by empty hotel rooms, even at the highest reaches of celebrity. Guitarist Pete Townshend of the Who describes the process that ends with "waking up in the morning with another few decibels of hearing gone":

First, getting excited. Doing exercises. Getting that fantastic adrenaline rush from a roar of people. And then looking down at your hand, and seeing that it's completely skinless and raw—this is in song number three—and you can't feel it. One is rather proud. You think, "Look what a great artist I am, what a cosmic performer!" Then the people are gone and they've paid their money and you're left with the wreckage. Which you have to live with. It's so brief, that moment on the stage. (38)

This passage will deter nobody from wanting that moment. But it also highlights one artist's suspicion about having to be crazy.

Clinging to the Myth

AND NOW WE come to the biggest reason the mad genius myth will never disappear: the public and press simply won't let it go. They must be crazy—because we like them that way.

The media's choice of what to cover, and how to position it, are absolutely crucial to the public's faith in the mad genius research. Although it galls me every time I see a headline about yet another allegedly crazy creative, I realize that, like sex, madness sells—the media can't be criticized for feeding the voracious appetite that already exists.

If a scientific study does blunder into the news cycle, it must be condensed into a short and snappy presentation. Here's what happened to one scientific expert on TV:

> This articulate, media-friendly man began a brief, lucid explanation of how he was planning to investigate and what evidence he would look for. But before he had spoken more than a few words, Larry King broke in impatiently to say, "Don't get technical, Professor, tell us what you believe!" (39)

If a story deserves more attention than this, producers will summon experts known for their strong opinions who will reliably reduce the issue to its most strident and simplistic terms. Nuance is about as useful to media outlets as it is in Congress. In the public arena, the mad genius has long since become a sound bite, with an empirical foundation as flimsy as Fantasyland—of course the Disney castle isn't real, but then you're not supposed to notice all the boards that are propping it up.

Celebrity Studies is a new journal that was supposed to promote the mad genius from pop mythology to legitimate academic concern. But its second issue turned tabloid with a series of essays on Michael Jackson's death—considering whether he was "freaky or fabulous" (40). It's unlikely that many stable celebrities will be studied, while the myth will keep getting a fresh coat of validation.

In the rare instances when credible new information does arrive to challenge the myth, it seems to slip under the radar. For example, Van Gogh's reputation as a great nut has already resisted every medical explanation for his behavior (such as the effects, singly or in combination, of epilepsy, absinthe, and syphilis). Yet there are now 819 of his letters easily available to the public—free and online—that reveal him to be remarkably sane and self-aware.

There is even evidence that it was actually his roommate and fellow painter Paul Gauguin who sliced off that famous lobe (41), and that Van Gogh's suicide was linked to the imminent death (from syphilis) of his beloved brother Theo, who was his only friend and supporter (42). So: bipolar disorder? Probably not.

Yet there's already been considerable professional resistance to the idea of a sane Van Gogh. Leo Jansen was one of three curators who prepared the letters for publication. When he was invited to share his new insights into Van Gogh's inner life at a bipolar conference, he wound up antagonizing the experts by challenging their favorite diagnosis. "I tried to look at all the facts in a more neutral way, and not follow the myth," he said, "[but] I was talking to deaf people" (43).

It's easy to understand why people cling to the old image of the helplessly crazy painter. Vincent's wild, whirling colors—and especially that self-portrait with bandaged ear—make him the perfect visual mascot for the mad genius idea. So damn the letters, full stereotype ahead!

Actually, it's time to slow down for some summary statements. As long as the creative path has so many hassles and heartbreaks, many will assume there must be something wrong with those who trudge it (they must be crazy). And despite the occasional boost from a Medici or a MacArthur grant, the basic reality is unlikely to change.

Besides, the myth will always be useful, since it converts any genius envy into pity, which is much less corrosive to the host. Our culture has nearly made an Olympic event out of "schadenfreude," the sport of enjoying someone else's misery or degradation. But we didn't invent it; there were also those spectators who paid to picnic at asylums so they could jeer and poke at the inmates—the very first reality show.

The myth also endures for the simple reason that there is no incentive to question it. The popular assumptions about crazy creatives are regularly confirmed by the media. In the professional world, while doubts flash like lightning bugs in the occasional article or chapter, it's rare to see any freestanding, strenuous objection to the creativity and madness link (before the book you're holding, the last dedicated volume appeared over twenty years ago). By now, the mad genius has rested so long on the comfy pillows of fact that it doesn't really matter whether it's presumed or real.

It's also fortified by the increasing cultural rush to embrace some mental glitch or other to excuse every failure in life. In many quarters, it's more popular to blame disappointment on a psychological disorder rather than on one's own bad choices. This can only support the idea that creatives are victims of their own psychology as well, an idea that some of them are happy to adopt and circulate.

Finally, nobody wants to abandon all that precious reassurance and compensation as well as spectacle. In Greek mythology, the prophets were blind; in modern mythology, the geniuses are pathological. That's why we embrace all the shabby pseudoscience we're offered: it "proves" what we so deeply need to believe: they must be crazy!

Coda

Let the bird sing without deciphering the song.
~ *Ralph Waldo Emerson*

THE MAD GENIUS IS A beloved cultural artifact, a popular spectacle, and a favorite playing-field leveler. It provides the perfect container for every romantic fantasy about both madness and genius—and doesn't have to be any more precise than that to be useful.

But a fact, it is not. There is simply no good reason to believe that exceptionally creative people are more afflicted with psychopathology than anyone else.

You may well disagree. Perhaps other writings, together with your own intuition and experience, have convinced you that creativity and madness do have a connection. That's your perfect right: I'm only asking you to give the tires a kick or two before you ride off in that particular vehicle.

Twiddling with Truth

HOWEVER, I DO expect a bit more from my colleagues in psychology and academia. Mostly, I wish they'd stop pretending they're doing science when their methods show so little respect for it. That would include diagnosing corpses with serious mental disorders based on gossip and hearsay from centuries past. Crucial practices like using randomized samples and considering possible sources of error variance have gone the way of other mathematical dodo birds, like adding up four numbers without having to use a calculator.

These days, many mental health practitioners express greater confidence about genetic linkages than do geneticists themselves. Some claim to represent a neuroscientific approach simply by using the word "brain," even if they've never gotten close enough to monitor one directly. Meanwhile, the core research principles of validity and reliability have taken their place in the Exhibit of Forgotten Necessities, together with that dusty rule about not starting with a conclusion and then manipulating everything else to fit it.

Despite their lofty aura, the terms "empirical" and "data" will not elevate the rigor of these efforts, any more than using the words "clinical," symptom," and "patient" turns a behavior problem into a disease. And the word "empirical" is so often confused with "experimental" that it hijacks its promise of precision, just as "significant result" is widely misunderstood to mean that something important has occurred.

Sadly, respect for research protocols is declining in general. The splinter Association for Psychological Science (APS) was created in 1988 by psychologists who found the original American Psychological Association too preoccupied with helping its members make a living. The APS publishes its own journals under the tattered banner of objectivity, while this APA continues to lobby for prescription privileges for psychologists—the money now being in drugs, rather than therapy.

The PsyD (Doctor of Psychology) degree, created in 1974 as a professional rather than academic credential, enables its graduates to practice psychology without having to endure years of statistics classes in order to design, conduct, and defend their own original experimental research. Such programs have more generous admission rates than PhDs, so despite their higher costs and student/faculty ratios, they have been proliferating like bunnies. The result is thousands of licensed clinicians who may be competent practitioners but are also less likely to notice that the mad genius is wobbling around on stilts (1).

In a related development, master's-level school psychologists were recently battling to retain their "psychologist" title without having to earn a doctoral degree like everyone else. This special exemption, granted thirty years ago, is now endangered by the ongoing turf wars in mental health. Trying to defend their unique privilege, their spokesperson argued that the only difference between a master's and a PhD was a dissertation and a couple of research courses: "not much," she said (2). Indeed. And alas.

Unfortunately, research details will always fall under the wheels of the snappy, confident conclusion, since nobody wants to hear about a study with tentative results. Given a world of twittering multitaskers who get pelted with stimuli from all sides—where everything is important, and therefore nothing is—you get just a few seconds to make your point and rise above the hive. That is not the moment to equivocate, even if that's all your study's results entitle you to do.

But that's quite enough finger wagging for one book. It's time to change the tune, raise the key, and talk about a more hopeful future.

Silver Linings

IT WOULD BE terrific if people would realize that creativity will always resist calibration, and that like a football coated with grease, genius will keep slipping out of our hands just when we think we've caught it. By now, it's clear that a full understanding of exceptional minds defies the soft tools of psychology—and is a quest more suited to literature, art, and philosophy. There's nothing wrong with quoting Poe and Byron, Dryden and Shakespeare, and anyone else with an interesting opinion on the matter—but we need to stop conflating that with science.

In any event, philosophy is where psychology has its deepest roots and greatest strength. This "love of wisdom" has always included pondering the Big Questions like, what is happiness? Love? Morality? And driving these abstract inquiries is the most urgent one of all: how do we make the best possible life with the cards we've been given?

Psychology used to lead these kinds of discussions, in line with its original mandate to hear the speech ("logo") of the soul ("psychi," or psee-HEE). The idea was to help people learn to listen to their own. But talk therapy has been double-teamed by the insurance and pharmaceutical industries—one restricting access to the process, and the other peddling a faster and easier solution. This leaves many psychologists, especially clinicians, wandering around in search of a new identity. And honestly? I don't think junior pill-pusher is it.

The good news is what's happening in the positive psychology movement. First kindled by Abraham Maslow and Carl Rogers in the 1960s, and later sparked into flame by Martin Seligman and Mihaly Csikszentmihalyi, this approach shifts the focus from everything that could ever go wrong with a human life to things like resilience and forgiveness, courage and optimism, and flow.

In 2004, Seligman and Christopher Peterson published *Character Strengths and Virtues,* their "un-DSM." This eight-hundred-page "manual of the sanities" is a handbook that might some day provide a parallel diagnostic system if mental health ever decides to switch from clouds to linings (3). And Seligman's *Flourish* (2011) not only proposes a more comprehensive view of happiness than found in his previous books, but also describes the extensive research and training that's been going on to bring it to more people.

These are the kind of pragmatic things psychologists should be doing, rather than wandering through Romantic poetry searching for science. And now there's yet another obstacle to understanding genius: the fact that the concept of exceptionalism itself has become muddy. When so many people are famous just for being famous, it throws the whole notion of real accomplishment out the virtual window.

And where does this leave us, at the end of our journey? Certainly better informed about the backstage doings of the mad genius, if not much closer to clarity. And now that the searchlight has clicked off and the path gone dark, we may as well get used to living with the mystery. This is less of a defeat than it seems—in fact, it's actually a sign of wisdom. In Maslow's famous hierarchy of needs, nobody makes it to absolute fulfillment—the very top of the psychological pyramid—without being able to tolerate ambiguity.

So as you close this book, please consider this: given all the anguish in the world, there are many serious questions that need psychology's urgent attention. I believe this focus will serve humanity far better than chasing its geniuses with a butterfly net and demeaning their work as the product of a disordered mind.

Notes

Prelude

1. Freedman 1985.
2. Brantley 2012.
3. Pickover 1998a; Eig 1998; *U.S. News & World Report*, May 21, 2001; Colt 2000, 51.
4. Roberts 2010; *Harvard Gazette* 2003; Ballie 2001, 17.
5. *The Simpsons* episode #442-2102, "Homer the Whopper," first airdate, September 27, 2009.
6. Osborne 2007.
7. Schlesinger 2002c.
8. Sudhalter 1999, 24.
9. Ratliff 2001, 32.
10. Jenkins 2008. In a personal communication in 2003, Gene Lees also enumerated some eminently sane jazz legends of his acquaintance, including Eddie "Lockjaw" Davis, Les McCann, Lou Levy, Clark Terry, Ed Thigpen, Hank Jones, John Lewis, and Dizzy Gillespie.
11. Lees 2001, 78.
12. Griffin in Taylor 1977, 69.
13. Rosen and Walter 2000, 237–44.
14. Margaret Helfgott 1998a, 1998b.
15. Friedman 2002.
16. Davis 2000.
17. Schlesinger 1998b, 2.
18. American Psychiatric Association 2007.
19. Spitzer 2011.
20. Foxhall 2001, 19.
21. Boxer, Burnett, and Swanson 1995; Kposowa 1999; Meltzer et. al 2008; Mustard et. al. 2010.

ONE: Creativity: Blind Men and Elephant Parts

1. Hershman and Lieb 1985, 11.
2. Sawyer 2006, 87.
3. Sternberg and Lubart 1995, 283.
4. Simonton 2004, 83–101.
5. Sternberg and Lubart 1996, 677.
6. Plucker, Beghetto, and Dow 2004, 90.
7. Sternberg, Kaufman, and Pretz 2002.
8. Westrup and Harrison 1985, 49.
9. Simonton 1994, 11.
10. Eysenck 1995, 287.
11. Frosch 1996, 507.
12. Freud [1922] 1965, 384.
13. Freud [1910] 1964, 25. It always amazes me how a man so thoroughly preoccupied with sex could give it up voluntarily when he turned forty, according to social historian Roy Porter (1989, 218), among others.
14. Landers 2000.
15. Byron, quoted in Marchand 1957, 894.
16. Artaud [1947] 1976, 492–93.
17. Nettle 2001, 141.
18. Rothenberg 1990, 8.
19. Czikszentmihalyi 1990, 1996, 1997.
20. Zeitlin, quoted in Sidran 1992, 400; Krieger 1994, personal communication.
21. Sternberg and Lubart 1995, 251.
22. Gardner 1993, 189.
23. Sawyer 2006, 130.
24. Sundararajan and Averill 2007.
25. Gordon and Bridglall 2005.
26. Hayes 1989.
27. Hennessey 2011.
28. Amabile et al. 2005, cited in Breen 2004.
29. Winner 2004, 2.
30. Csikszentmihalyi 1996, 58–73; Wallace 1989; Von Karolyi and Winner 2005, 279; Amabile 2001, 335.
31. Amabile et al. 2005, 397–98.
32. Gelb 1998.
33. Richards 2009; Weisberg 1993; 2006; Sternberg et al. 1996, 352.
34. Gardner, quoted in Shekerjian 1990, 141.

35. Storr 1993, xiii, 93.
36. Storr 1992, 113.
37. Freud, quoted in Arieti 1976, 23.
38. Juni, Nelson, and Brannon 1987.
39. Meyer 1956, 222.
40. Mitchell and McDonald 2009.
41. Hayden 2003; Worthen 2007.
42. Shapero 1985, 42.
43. Seashore 1938, 2; born in Sweden in 1866 as a Sjostrand, the name was changed in 1870, when the family moved to Iowa. "Seashore" is its literal English equivalent.
44. Kemp 1996.
45. Seashore 1938, 32.
46. Derbyshire 2003.
47. Kemp 1996, 174–75.
48. Deutsch 1982; Sloboda 1985; Aiello 1994.
49. Sloboda and Juslin 2001, 73.
50. Copland 1952, 51.
51. Hargreaves and North 1998.
52. Stolorow and Atwood 1979, 18.
53. Christopher Lehmann-Haupt 2001.
54. Adler, quoted in May 1975, 43.
55. Richards 2009.
56. Richards 1992, 5.
57. Koch, quoted in Franklin 2001, 446.
58. Bernstein 1982, 232.

TWO: Elastic Madness: One Size Fits All

1. Thomas and Mitchum 2010, 9.
2. Lane 2007, 114.
3. Kagan 2008.
4. DSM IV 1994, 83–84.
5. Thomas 2004, 1.
6. Harris 2008a.
7. More Information about Dr. Joseph Biederman in Harris 2008b; see also "What Killed Rebecca Riley?" *60 Minutes* video, 2007, and anything else on the reference list by Harris and the other fine *New York Times* science

reporters Benedict Carey and Janet Roberts. Also helpful: Schlesinger 2002d; Kowalczyk, 2009; Whitaker 2005. For the impact of drug-pushing ads on rates of diagnosis, see Lacasse 2005.

8. Frances 2010, 2009.
9. Hyman 2011.
10. Kutchins and Kirk 1997; Caplan 1995; Caplan and Cosgrove 2004; for the transformation of shyness into a mental illness, which incorporates many of the same DSM shenanigans ten years later, see Lane 2007.
11. President's New Freedom Commission 2003; American Psychiatric Association 2003.
12. Ibid.
13. Mischel 2009.
14. Begley 2009.
15. Sleek 1996, 30.
16. Eysenck 1995, 214.
17. Beutler 2000, 999; Baker et al. 2008, 80; Essau 2004, 117.
18. Kim and Ahn 2002.
19. Faust and Ziskin 1988, 31.
20. Akiskal 2000, 5–6.
21. DSM-IV 1994, 332.
22. Ratey and Johnson 1997, 14.
23. American Psychiatric Association 2010a.
24. Copland, quoted in Frosch 1987, 320.
25. Rothenberg 1990, 39.
26. Zhong, Dijksterhuis, and Galinsky 2008; Kounios and Jung-Beeman 2009.
27. Czikszentmihalyi 1996, 58.
28. Koch, quoted in Franklin 2001, 450.
29. Shekerjian 1990, xxii.
30. Rothenberg 1990, 15.
31. Plucker and Makel 2010, 1.
32. Horwitz 2002, 20.
33. Diamond 1975, 223.
34. Smith 2007.

THREE: Melancholy Becomes Romantic

1. Plato 2002, 25–27.
2. Kris and Kurz 1979, 113.
3. Aristotle 1984, bk. 30, 1501, lines 39–41.

4. Northwood 2010.

5. Aristotle 1984, bk. 30, 1502, lines 30–40.

6. Anglicus (in 1470), quoted in Hunter and Macalpine 1982, 1.

7. Du Laurens (in 1597), ibid., 51.

8. Aristotle 1984, bk. 3, pt. 1.

9. Seneca, n.d.

10. Padel 1995, 30.

11. Plato 2002, 33.

12. Rosen 1969, 103.

13. Padel 1995, 3.

14. Bartlett 1992, 119.

15. Wittkower 1963, 1.

16. Cantor 1994, 477.

17. Ibid., 289–94.

18. Just for the record, the first dated Chinese book appeared in AD 868.

19. Radden 2000, 81, 83, 84.

20. Ibid., 89.

21. Wittkowers 1963, 103.

22. Radden 2000, 14.

23. Kris and Kurz 1979, 49.

24. An extensive and detailed critique of this list appears in Schlesinger 2009, 66–67.

25. Johnson 2000, 79.

26. Ibid., 147.

27. Ibid., 146–47.

28. Foucault 1965, 127.

29. Skultans 1979, 38.

30. Foucault 1965, 157.

31. Monroe 1992, 234.

32. Foucault 1965, 90.

33. Burton (in 1621), quoted in Bartlett 1992, 94, 96–97. The full *The Anatomy of Melancholy* can be accessed free and online at Project Gutenberg.

34. Barrough (in 1583), noted in Hunter and Macalpine 1982, 28.

35. Rosen 1969, 165.

36. Skultans 1979, 38.

37. Foucault 1965, 221.

38. Another version was called Dr. Cox's Circulating Swing. See also Hunter and Macalpine 1963, under Joseph Mason Cox, "A Herculean Remedy: The Swing," 594–98; Dr. Cox noted that vomiting was "esteemed" as one of the most successful remedies for madness.

39. William Wordsworth 1802, "My Heart Leaps Up When I Behold," in Perkins 1967, 279.

40. Keats 1819, "Ode on a Grecian Urn," in Perkins 1967, 1186.

41. Ibid., "I Cry Your Mercy," in Perkins 1967, 1204.

42. Shaw 1931, 84–85.

43. Washington 1995.

44. Percy Bysshe Shelley (in 1820), "To a Skylark," lines 101–5, in Washington 1995, 1035.

45. Macaulay [1825] 1891, 6.

46. Poe (in 1842), "Eleanora," cited in Becker 1978, 58.

47. Porter 2002, 86.

48. Perkins 1967, 953.

FOUR: The Rise of Righteous Rumor

1. Becker 1978, 77.

2. Cooper, Report on Lunacy 1844.

3. Moreau du Tours, quoted in Becker 1978, 79.

4. Nisbet 1891, vi.

5. Kessel 1989, 199.

6. Galton 1892, ix–x.

7. Porter 2002, 183.

8. Lombroso 1895, 5–37, vi.

9. Grinder 1985, 13.

10. Andreasen 1987, 1289.

11. Jamison 1993, 53.

12. "Guiteaumania" 1882, 948.

13. Storr 1993, 116.

14. Nisbet 1891, vi, 316–17.

15. Jamison 1993, 125–26.

16. Wittkowers 1963, 287.

17. Huneker 1900, 76 (emphasis mine); Liszt [1857] 1963, 84.

18. Hyslop 1925, 233, 219, 228.

19. Trombley 1981, 227.

20. Hyslop 1925, 271, 275.

21. Schlesinger 2002b, 140.

22. Freud 1956; Choisy 1955.

23. *The Merchant of Venice*, act 5, sc. 1, lines 83–88, in Shakespeare 1974, 353.

24. Esquirol 1845, 39.

25. James 1902, 343, 24.

26. Ellis 1904, 191.

27. Ellis (in 1927), cited in Becker 1978, 41.

28. Lange-Eichbaum 1932, 24, 27; Loewenberg 1950, 927.

29. Lange-Eichbaum, quoted in Becker 1978, 90.

30. Eysenck 1995, 19.

31. Juda 1949, 84.

32. Menninger, quoted in Porter 2002, 208.

33. Hinshaw 2007, x.

34. Corrigan and Penn 1999, 765–66.

35. Neugeboren 1999, 141.

FIVE: Premature Victories

1. ISAD 2005.

2. Lubin et al. 1988, 136.

3. Genetic research project, University of Pittsburgh, Department of Human Genetics. 1999.

4. Sachs 2001, personal communication.

5. Schlesinger 2010.

6. Ibid., 2009.

7. Andreasen 2005, 93.

8. Holden 1987.

9. *Science News*, October 24, 1987.

10. Andreasen 1987, 1289; also at Axinn Conference 1986.

11. Gutin 1996.

12. Jamison 1989, 126.

13. For example, Andreasen studied 27 men and 3 women. Jamison says that 87 percent of her sample of 47 were men, or 40.89 males. The "fractional man" is not explained.

14. Just a few commenders: Richards 1992, 4; Nettle 2001, 142–43; Anderegg and Gartner 2001, 366.

15. Jamison 1995a, 16.

16. Jamison 1989, 126.

17. Jamison 2005, 225; 2002, 2.

18. Sarbin and Mancuso 1980, 32.

19. Lish et al. 1994, 288.

20. Jamison 1989, 133.

21. Rothenberg 1990, 8.

22. Ibid., 150–53.
23. Jamison 1993, 300–301.
24. Ibid., 59.
25. Jamison 2004b; Merkin 2004b.
26. Jamison 2003.
27. Flaherty 2004, 32.
28. Nesse 1998, 6.
29. Jamison 1998; 2004a, 126.
30. Feist 2001, 13.
31. Jamison 1993, 5.
32. Schlesinger 2009, 2010.
33. Jamison 1993, 221–22.
34. Ibid., 168, 199.
35. Blake (in 1800), letter to William Hayley, quoted in Perkins 1967, 164.
36. Perkins 1967, 38.
37. Blake, cited in Perkins 1967, 41.
38. Jamison 1993, 268.
39. Gelder 2001.
40. Silvia and Kaufman 2010, 383.
41. Schlesinger 2009.
42. Ludwig 1995, 5, 7, 35, 49, 157.
43. Keynes 1980; Jamison 1989a; Sandblom 1997, 39–40.
44. Frosch 1989, 767; 1999, 41, 53.
45. Hayden 2003; Worthen 2007.
46. Simonton 2004, 37.
47. Hayden 2003, 314.
48. Szasz 2006, 99.
49. James 1994, 27.
50. Casey 2002, 3.
51. Jamison 1995b, 217–18.

SIX: Blunt Tools and Slippery Slopes

1. This problem also applies to other ambiguous variables that keep showing up in this research, like "latent inhibition," "schizotypy," and the whole realm of giftedness, but they're for someone else to wrestle with.
2. Schwarz 1999.
3. Lish et al. 1994.
4. Azar 1997.

5. Kerlinger 1973, 681.
6. Joseph 2004, 231.
7. "Vincent van Gogh Mad Genius Gene" 2009; Roberts 2010.
8. Oliver and Simmons 1985, 470.
9. Schulze 2010, 76.
10. Cohen 2011.
11. *Tuberculosis and Genius* book review in the *New York Times*, May 13, 1909; *Journal of the American Medical Association*, 1941; *Journal of Nervous and Mental Diseases*, 1942.
12. Hayden 2003, 107.
13. Post 1994, 27.
14. Ibid., 32.
15. Maisel 2008, 19; Wittkower and Wittkower 1963, 292.
16. Jamison 1993, 199, 168.
17. Simonton 1994, 288.
18. Janofsky 1997.
19. Kessel 1989, 90.
20. Friedman 2011.
21. Ludwig 1995, 171.
22. Sandke 2010.
23. Storr 1993, 144.
24. Shaffer 2000.
25. Sandblom 1997, 73–75.
26. Jamison 1993, 298; 1998.
27. Wills 2003, 258.
28. Ibid., 257.
29. Ibid., 259.
30. Wills 2004, 185.
31. Runyan 1981.
32. Runyan 1982, 445.
33. Wills 2004, 185.
34. Schlesinger 2004b, 364.
35. Storr 1993, 138.
36. Frosch 1987, 322.
37. Woods 1911, 2.
38. Simonton 1990, 17–18.
39. Ibid., 148.
40. Simonton 1986, 155.
41. Ibid., 151.
42. Ibid., 153.

43. Ibid.
44. Simonton 1990, 38.
45. *A Midsummer Night's Dream*, act 5, sc. 1, lines 7–17, in Shakespeare [1594–1595] 1992, 54.
46. *Absalom and Architophel*, lines 163–70, in Dryden [1681] 2004, 5–6.
47. Marchand 1957, 894, 932.
48. Jamison 1993, 2.
49. Thackeray, quoted in Perkins 1967, 786.
50. Perkins 1967, 781.
51. Mayne 1910, 139.
52. Hyslop 1925, 249.
53. Marchand 1957, xiii.
54. Grosskurth 1997, 56, 79, 307, 109; Schlesinger 1997a.
55. Sachs 2010, 44.
56. Ibid.
57. Ibid., 43–44.
58. Tim O'Brien at Axinn Memorial Conference 1986.

SEVEN: Awesome Powers

Epigraph. Sarton [1965] 1993, 169.
1. Sondheim 1998.
2. Styron 1990, 66–67.
3. Sloboda 1992, 34–35.
4. Burton [1621] 2001, 116–17.
5. Hart and Lieberman 1991, 42.
6. Rouget 1985, 122.
7. Clynes 1982, 54, 66, 80.
8. Blood and Zatorre 2001, 11823; "This Is Your Brain on Jazz" 2008.
9. Collier, quoted in Crofton and Frasier 1985, 56.
10. Rouget 1985, 13–14.
11. Simonton 1994, 211.
12. Foucault 1965, 177–79.
13. Hanser 1983, 5.
14. Bergman, quoted in Lahr 1999, 72.
15. Kris and Kurz 1979, 89–90.
16. Pianist Karl Ulrich Schnabel, *New York Times*, January 16, 1994.
17. Berg 2007.
18. Kris and Kurz 1979, 129.

19. Smith 2004, 52; Schlesinger 1999a.
20. Hennessey and Amabile 1998, 674.
21. Goldstein 1980.
22. Van de Ven, Zeelenberg, and Pieters 2010; *Daily Mail Reporter*, 2010.
23. Schlesinger 2003.
24. Fischer 2001.
25. Hanna-Plady and MacKay 2011; Arnold 2011.
26. Kessel 1989, 203.
27. Lees 1999, 6.
28. Eysenck 1997, 264.
29. Szasz 1987, 226.
30. Eysenck 1995, 245.
31. Ibid, 235.
32. Hamilton and Cairn 1973, 665–66.
33. Rouget 1985, 231.
34. Waldman 2001, 7; Taruskin 2001, 1.
35. Published in the *New York American*, June 22, 1922.
36. Gural 2000.
37. Rhead 2004, 220.

EIGHT: They Must Be Crazy

1. Kris and Kurz 1979, 114.
2. NEA 2002, 5.
3. Fishman 2002, personal communication.
4. Wright 2004, personal communication.
5. Gedo 1996, 159–60.
6. Clark 1998, personal communication.
7. Rouget 1985, 216.
8. Sonneck 1926, 25; Menuhin and David 1979, 149.
9. Einstein 1986, 13.
10. Lebrecht 1982, 30.
11. Bernstein 1959, 57.
12. Alexander 1998.
13. Plucker and Levy 2001, 75.
14. Berg 2010.
15. Gedo 1996, 160.
16. Allen 1997, 1998, personal communications.
17. Solis 2004.

18. Kelley 2009, xvii.
19. Freedman 1985.
20. Egner 1996, personal communication.
21. Israels 2001, personal communication.
22. Becker 1978, 57–58.
23. Martindale 1998, 8.
24. Hentoff 1991, 54.
25. Lees 1987, 41.
26. Becker 1978, 10.
27. Freedman 1985.
28. Rehak 1999.
29. Zaslow 1996.
30. Gardner 1993, 368.
31. Frishberg 2004, personal communication.
32. Frishberg and Dorough 1964.
33. Becker 1973, 85, 87, 100.
34. Shaw in May 1975, 27.
35. Weisberg 1993, 39.
36. Mercer, quoted in Lees 1987, 46–47.
37. Washburne 2004, 132, 143.
38. Townshend, quoted in Gates 1989, 67.
39. Naughton 2001, 19.
40. Bennett 2010, 232.
41. Crisafis 2009; Gopnik 2010.
42. Gedo 1996, 83.
43. Taylor 2007; Van Gogh letters at www.vangoghletters.org.

Coda

1. Baker, McFall, and Shoham 2009, 85.
2. Bradshaw 2008, 1.
3. Seligman and Peterson 2004; Seligman 2011a, 2011b.

References

Abramson, John. 2005. *Overdo$ed America: The Broken Promise of American Medicine*. New York: Harper Perennial Books.

Abuhamdeh, Sami, and Mihaly Csikszentmihalyi. 2004. "The Artistic Personality: A Systems Perspective." In *Creativity: From Potential to Realization*, edited by Robert J. Sternberg, Elena L. Grigorenko, and Jerome L. Singer, 31–42. Washington, DC: American Psychological Association.

Aiello, Rita, ed., with John A. Sloboda. 1993. *Musical Perceptions*. New York: Oxford University Press.

Akiskal, Hagop S. 2000. "Temperament and Mood Disorders." *Harvard Mental Health Letter* 16 (8): 5–6.

Alexander, Monty, 1998. Personal communication, December 11.

Allen, Richard C., Elyce Zenoff Ferster, and Jesse G. Rubin, eds. 1975. *Readings in Law and Psychiatry*. Baltimore: Johns Hopkins University Press.

Allen, Steve. 1997. Personal communication, February 3.

———. 1998. Personal communication, June 30.

Amabile, Teresa M. 1996. *Creativity in Context*. Boulder, CO: Westview Press.

———. 1998. "Reward, Intrinsic Motivation, and Creativity." *American Psychologist* 53 (6): 1241–47.

———. 2001. "Beyond Talent: John Irving and the Passionate Craft of Creativity," *American Psychologist* 56 (5): 333–36.

Amabile, Teresa M., Sigal G. Barsade, Jennifer S. Mueller, and Barry M. Shaw. 2005. "Affect and Creativity at Work," *Administrative Science Quarterly* 50: 367–403.

American Psychiatric Association. 1994. *Diagnostic and Statistical Manual of Mental Disorders (DSM)*. 4th ed. Washington, DC.

———. 2003. Press Release 03–39: "Statement on Diagnosis and Treatment of Mental Disorders," September 26. http://www.psych.org/MainMenu/Newsroom/NewsReleases/2003NewsReleases.

———. 2007. "DSM-V Task Force and Work Group Acceptance Form."

Accessed March 15, 2011. http://www.psych.org/MainMenu/Research/
DSMIV/DSMV/BOTPrinciples/DSMMemberAcceptanceForm.aspx.

———. 2010a. "DSM Development: Attenuated Psychosis Syndrome." Accessed August 16, 2011. http://www.dsm5.org/ProposedRevisions/Pages/
proposedrevision.aspx?rid=412.

———. 2010b. FAQs: "What's So 'Statistical' about the Diagnostic and Statistical Manual of Mental Disorders?" Accessed March 14, 2011. http://www
.psych.org/MainMenu/Research/DSMIV/FAQs.

Amram, David. 2009. Personal communication, August 31.

Anderegg, David, and Gina Gartner. 2001. "Manic Dedifferentiation and the
Creative Process." *Psychoanalytic Psychology* 18 (2): 265–379.

Andreasen, Nancy C. 1987. "Creativity and Mental Illness: Prevalence Rates in
Writers and Their First-Degree Relatives." *American Journal of Psychiatry*
144: 1288–92.

———. 2005. *The Creating Brain: The Neuroscience of Genius.* New York: The
Dana Foundation.

Arieti, Silvano. 1976. Creativity: *The Magic Synthesis.* New York: Basic Books.

Aristotle 1984. *Problemata.* In *The Complete Works of Aristotle: The Revised Oxford
Translation*, vol. 2, edited by Jonathan Barnes, 1319–1527. Princeton, NJ:
Princeton University Press.

Arnold, Carrie. 2011. "Musicians Stay Sharp." *Scientific American*, August 31.
http://www.scientificamerican.com/article.cfm?id=musicians-stay-sharp.

Artaud, Antonin. (1947) 1976. *Van Gogh, the Man Suicided by Society.* Selected
Writings. Edited and with an introduction by Susan Sontag. Berkeley,
CA: University of California Press. 483–512.

Axinn, Michael M. Annual Memorial Conference. 1986. "Mood Disorders and Their Effect on Creativity." North Shore University Hospital,
Manhasset, NY, May 2.

Azar, Beth. 1997. "Poor Recall Mars Research and Treatment: Inaccurate
Self-Reports Can Lead to Faulty Research Conclusions and Inappropriate
Treatment." *APA Monitor on Psychology* 28 (1): 1–3.

Baker, Timothy B., Richard M. McFall, and Varda Shoham. 2009. "Current
Status and Future Prospects of Clinical Psychology: Toward a Scientifically Principled Approach to Mental and Behavioral Health Care." *Psychological Science in the Public Interest* 9 (2): 67–103.

Ballie, R. 2001. "The Melody behind Mental Illness?" *APA Monitor on Psychology* 31 (10): 17.

Barnes, Jonathan, ed. 1984. *The Complete Works of Aristotle: The Revised Oxford
Translation.* Vol. 2. Princeton, NJ: Princeton University Press.

Barrough, Philip. 1583. "On the Frenisie, Lethargy, Apoplexy, Epilepsia, Madnes and Melancholie" [sic]. In Hunter and Macalpine 1982, 24–28.

Bartlett, John. 1992. *Bartlett's Familiar Quotations*. 16th ed. Edited by Justin Kaplan. New York: Little, Brown and Company.

Becker, George. 1978. *The Mad Genius Controversy: A Study in the Sociology of Deviance*. London: Sage Publications.

Becker, Howard G. 1973. *Outsiders: Studies in the Sociology of Deviance*. New York: The Free Press.

Begley, Sharon. 2009. "Ignoring the Evidence: Why Do Psychologists Reject Science?" *Newsweek*, October 12. http://newsweek.com/id/216506.

Bennett, James. 2010. "Michael Jackson: Celebrity Death, Mourning, and Media Events." *Celebrity Studies* 1 (2): 231–32.

Benolken, Sarah, and Colin Martindale, eds. 2000. "Special Issue: Creativity and Psychopathology." *Bulletin of Psychology and the Arts*. Washington, DC: American Psychological Association Division 10, 1 (2).

Berg, Shelly. 2007. Lecture on the M/S Westerdam somewhere on the Caribbean Sea, November 13.

———. 2010. Personal communication, April 8.

Bernstein, Leonard. 1959. *The Joys of Music*. New York: Simon & Schuster.

Beutler, Larry. 2000. "David and Goliath: When Empirical and Clinical Standards of Practice Meet." *American Psychologist* 55 (9): 997–1007.

Blader, J. C., and G. A. Carlson. 2007. "Increased Rates of Bipolar Disorder Diagnoses among U.S. Child, Adolescent, and Adult Populations, 1996–2004." *Biological Psychiatry* 62: 107–14.

Blakeslee, Sandra. 1995. "The Mystery of Music: How It Works in the Brain." *New York Times*, Science section, May 16, C1 and C10.

Blood, A. J., and R. J. Zatorre. 2001. "Intensely Pleasurable Responses to Music Correlate with Activity in Brain Regions Implicated with Reward and Emotion." *Proceedings of the National Academy of Sciences* 98 (20): 11818–23.

Boxer, P. A., Burnett, C., and N. Swanson. 1995. "Suicide and occupation: A review of the literature." Journal of Occupational and Environmental Medicine 37 (4): 442–52.

Bradshaw, James. 2008. "School Psychologists Fight to Keep Title." *National Psychologist* 17 (1): 3.

———. 2009. "Concerns Voiced over Secrecy Surrounding DSM-V." *National Psychologist* 18 (3). http://nationalpsychologist.com.

Brantley, Ben. 2012. "A Star Was Born, Sparkled, and Fell." *New York Times*, Theater Reviews, April 2. http://theater.nytimes.com/2012/04/03/theater/reviews/end-of-the-rainbow-on-judy-garland-at-belasco-theater.html.

Breen, Bill. 2004. "The 6 Myths of Creativity." Interview with Teresa Amabile. FastCompany.com. (89), December 19. http://www.fastcompany.com/magazine/89/creativity.html.

Breggin, Peter R. 2008. "800,000 'Bipolar Children.'" *Ethical Human Psychology and Psychiatry* 10 (2): 67–70.

Builione, R. Scott, and Jack P. Lipton. 1983. "Stereotypes and Personality of Classical Musicians." *Psychomusicology* 3 (1): 36–43.

Burnham, Scott, and Michael P. Steinberg, eds. 2000. *Beethoven and His World.* Princeton, NJ: Princeton University Press.

Burton, Robert. (1621) 2001. *The Anatomy of Melancholy, What It Is: With All the Kinds, Causes, Symptoms, Prognostickes, and Severall Cures of It.* Introduction by William H. Gass. New York: New York Review of Books.

Cantor, Norman F. 1994. *The Civilization of the Middle Ages: A Completely Revised and Expanded Edition of Medieval History: The Life and Death of a Civilization.* New York: Harper Perennial.

Caplan, Paula J. 1995. *They Say You're Crazy: How the World's Most Powerful Psychiatrists Decide Who's Normal.* Reading, Massachusetts: Addison-Wesley.

Caplan, Paula J., and Lisa Cosgrove, eds. 2004. *Bias in Psychiatric Diagnosis.* Lanham, MD: Rowman and Littlefield.

Carey, Benedict. 2007a. "Bipolar Illness Soars as a Diagnosis for the Young." *New York Times*, September 4. http://www.nytimes.com/2007/09/04/health/04psych.html.

———. 2007b. "Debate over Children and Psychiatric Drugs." *New York Times*, February 15.

———. 2010. "Popular Drugs May Help Only Severe Depression." *New York Times*, January 6, A12.

Cartwright, Samuel. 1851. "Diseases and Peculiarities of the Negro Race." In *De Bow's Review of the Southern and Western States, Devoted to Commerce, Agriculture, Manufactures, Internal Improvements, Statistics, General Literature &c*, vol. 11, edited by J. D. B. de Bow, 331–33. Making of America Project. Google Books.

Casey, Nell, ed. 2002. *Unholy Ghost: Writers on Depression.* New York: Harper Perennial.

Channing, Walter. 1900. "Stigma of Degeneration: The Case of Amos D. Palmer." Read at a meeting of the Boston Medico-Psychological Society, November 9, 1989. *American Journal of Insanity* 4: 615–24.

Choisy, Maryse. (1955) 1973. "Memories of My Visits with Freud." In *Freud as We Knew Him*, edited by Hendrik M. Ruitenbeek, 291–95. Detroit: Wayne State University Press.

Chrisafis, Angelique. 2009. "Art Historians Claim Van Gogh's Ear Cut Off by Gauguin." *Guardian*. http://www.guardian.co.uk/artanddesign/2009/may/04/vincent-van-gogh-ear.

Clark, Graham. 1998. Personal communication, March 15.

Clynes, Manfred. 1982. *Music, Mind, and Brain: The Neuropsychology of Music.* New York: Springer Publishing.

———. 1989. *Sentics: The Touch of the Emotions.* Dorset, England: Prism Press.

———. 2010. Personal communication, November 13.

Cohen, David, and Keith Hoeller. 2003. "Screening for Depression: Preventive Medicine or Telemarketing?" Ethical Human Sciences and Services 5 (1): 3–6.

Cohen, Patricia. 2011. "Genetic Basis for Crime: A New Look." *New York Times*, June 20, C1.

Colt, Jonathan. 2000. "God, Man, and the Media: Deepak Chopra." *Rolling Stone*, September 28, 47–51.

Columbia Bipolar Genetic Study. Online and ongoing. http://bipolar.hs.columbia.edu/disgenet.htm.

Comini, Alessandra. 2000. "The Visual Beethoven: Whence, Why, and Whither the Scowl?" In *Beethoven and His World*, edited by Scott Burnham and Michael P. Steinberg, 287–312. Princeton, NJ: Princeton University Press.

Cooper, Anthony Ashley. 1844. "Report of the Metropolitan Commissioners in Lunacy, to the Lord Chancellor, Presented to Both Houses of Parliament by Command of Her Majesty." In Hunter and Macalpine 1982, 923–30.

Copland, Aaron. 1939. *What to Listen for in Music.* New York: McGraw-Hill Book Company.

———. 1952. *Music and Imagination.* Cambridge: Harvard University Press.

Corrigan, Patrick. 2004. "How Stigma Interferes with Mental Health Care." *American Psychologist* 59 (7): 614–25.

Corrigan, Patrick W., and David L. Penn. 1999. "Lessons from Social Psychology on Discrediting Psychiatric Stigma." *American Psychologist* 54 (9): 765–73.

Cox, Joseph Mason. 1804. "A Herculean Remedy: The Swing." In Hunter and Macalpine 1982, 596–98.

Croarkin, Paul. 2002. "From King George to Neuroglobin: The Psychiatric Aspects of Acute Intermittent Porphyria." *Journal of Psychiatric Practice* 8 (6): 398–405.

Crofton, Ian, and Donald Fraser. 1985. *A Dictionary of Musical Quotations.* New York: Schirmer Books.

Cromie, William J. 2003. "The Links Between Creativity, Intelligence, and

Mental Illness: Irrelevance Can Make You Mad." *Harvard University Gazette*, October 23. http://news.harvard.edu/gazette/story/2003/10/the-links-between-creativity-intelligence-and-mental-illness.

Czikszentmihalyi, Mihaly. 1990. *Flow: The Psychology of Optimal Experience: Steps Toward Enhancing the Quality of Life*. New York: Harper & Row.

———. 1996. *Creativity: Flow and the Psychology of Discovery and Invention*. New York: HarperCollins.

———. 1997. *Finding Flow: The Psychology of Engagement with Everyday Life*. New York: Basic Books.

Davis, Clive. 2000. "He Died a Fallen Idol, But Chet Baker Is Set for a Revival Thanks to Hollywood." *London Times*, February 27.

Derbyshire, David. 2003. "It Helps to Be Mad in the Jazz World." *London Daily Telegraph*, February 9.

Deutsch, Diana, ed. 1982. *The Psychology of Music*. New York: Academic Press.

Diamond, Bernard L. 1975. "The Fallacy of the Impartial Expert." In Allen et al. 1975, 217–25.

Dryden, John (1681) 2004. *Absalom and Architophel*. Pt. 1. Reprint edition, Whitefish: MT: Kessinger Publishing's Rare Reprints. Google Books.

Dulzo, Jim. 2002. "Music, Mental Illness, Prison, and Drummer Roy Brooks." *JazzTimes*, October.

Egner, Richard E. 1996. Personal communication, December 18.

Eig, Jonathan. 1998. "Tom Harrell: Like Night and Day." *Esquire*, December. http://www.shout.net/~jmh/articles/harrell01.html.

Einstein, Alfred. 1986. *Greatness in Music*. New York: Da Capo.

Ellis, Havelock. 1904. *A Study of British Genius*. London: Hurst & Blackwell. Google Books.

Esquirol, Jean-Etienne Dominique. 1845. *Mental Maladies: A Treatise on Insanity*. Translated from the French, with additions, by E. K. Hunt, MD. Philadelphia: Lea and Blanchard. Google Books.

Essau, Cecelia A. 2004. "Vulnerability Factors of Psychopathology across the Life Span." *Contemporary Psychology APA Review of Books* 49 (1): 117–19.

Eysenck, Hans. 1995. *Genius: The Natural History of Creativity*. New York: Cambridge University Press.

———. 1997. *Rebel with a Cause: The Autobiography of Hans Eysenck*. New Brunswick, NJ: Transaction Publishers.

Faust, David, and Jay Ziskin. 1988. "The Expert Witness in Psychology and Psychiatry." *Science*, 241, 31–35.

Feist, Gregory J. 2001. "Natural and Sexual Selection in the Evolution of Creativity." *American Psychological Association Bulletin of Psychology and the Arts* 2 (1): 11–16.

Fischer, Clare. 2001. Personal communication, June 16.

Fishman, Greg. 2002. Personal communication, April 9.

Fitzgerald, G., and J. A. Hattie. 1983. "An Evaluation of the 'Your Style of Learning and Thinking' Inventory." *British Journal of Educational Psychology* 53 (3): 336–46.

Flaherty, Alice W. 2004. *The Midnight Disease: The Drive to Write, Writer's Block, and the Creative Brain.* Boston: Houghton Mifflin.

Foucault, Michael. 1965. *Madness and Civilization: A History of Insanity in the Age of Reason.* Translated from the French by Richard Howard. New York: Vintage Books.

Foxhall, K. 2001. "Suicide by Profession: Lots of Confusion, Inconclusive Data." *Monitor on Psychology* 32 (1): 19.

Frances, Allen. 2009. "A Warning Sign on the Road to DSM-5: Beware of Its Unintended Consequences." *Psychiatric Times* 26 (8). http://www.psychiatric times.com/print/article/10168/1425378.

———. 2010. "The DSM 5 Field Trials, Part 2: Asking the Wrong Questions Will Lead to Irrelevant Answers." PsychologyToday.com, November 23.

Franklin, Margery B. 2001. "The Artist Speaks: Sigmund Koch on Aesthetics and Creative Work." *American Psychologist* 56 (5): 445–52.

Freedman, Samuel G. 1985. "How Inner Torment Feeds the Creative Spirit." *New York Times*, November 17.

Freud, Harry. (1956) 1973. "My Uncle Sigmund." In *Freud as We Knew Him*, edited by Hendrick M. Ruitenbeek, 313. Detroit: Wayne State U. Press.

Freud, Sigmund. (1910) 1964. *Leonardo da Vinci and a Memory of His Childhood.* Translated by Alan Tyson. New York: W. W. Norton.

———. (1922) 1965. *A General Introduction to Psychoanalysis.* Authorized English translation of the revised edition by Joan Riviere. New York: Washington Square Press.

Friedman, Richard A. 2002. "Connecting Depression and Artistry." *New York Times*, Health section, June 4.

———. 2011. "How a Telescopic Lens Muddles Psychiatric Insights." *New York Times*, May 24, D5.

Frishberg, Dave. 2004. Personal communication, April 6.

Frishberg, Dave, and Bob Dorough. 1964. "I'm Hip." Used by permission of Swiftwater Music and Aral Music.

Frosch, William A. 1987. "Moods, Madness, and Music: 1. Major Affective Disease and Musical Creativity." *Comprehensive Psychiatry* 28 (4): 315–22.

———. 1989. "The 'Case' of George Frideric Handel." *New England Journal of Medicine* 321 (11): 765–69. Accessed March 20, 2008. http://gfhandel.org/ frosch.html.

————. 1990. "Moods, Madness, and Music. II. Was Handel Insane?" *The Musical Quarterly* 74 (1): 31–56.

————. 1996. "Creativity: Is There a Worm in the Apple?" *Journal of the Royal Society of Medicine* 89 (September): 506–8.

Galton, Francis. 1892. *Hereditary Genius: An Inquiry into Its Laws and Consequences*. 2nd ed. London: Macmillan & Co. http://galton.org/books.

Gardner, Howard. 1993. *Creating Minds: An Anatomy of Creativity Seen through the Lives of Freud, Einstein, Picasso, Stravinsky, Eliot, Graham, and Gandhi*. New York: Basic Books.

Gates, David. 1989. "See Them! Feel Them! The Who's Back, Again." *Newsweek*, July 3.

Gay, Peter. 1988. *Freud: A Life for Our Time*. New York: W. W. Norton.

Gedo, John E. 1996. *The Artist and the Emotional World: Creativity and Personality*. New York: Columbia University Press.

Geeves, Andrew, and Doris McIlwain. 2009. "That Blissful Feeling: Phenomenological Conceptions of Music Performance from One Performer's Perspective." In Aaron Williamon et al. 2009, 415–20.

Gelb, Michael J. 2002. *How to Think Like Leonardo da Vinci: Seven Steps to Genius Every Day*. New York: Dell.

Gelder, Michael. 2001. Anthony Storr Obituary. *Independent*, March 23. http://www.independent.co.uk/news/obituaries/anthony-storr-728955. html.

Ghiselin, Brewster, ed. 1985. *The Creative Process: A Symposium*. Berkeley, CA: University of California Press.

Glater, Jonathan D. 2004. "Joyously Watching Others Fail." *New York Times*, February 29, 6.

Glennie, Evelyn. 1993. "Hearing Essay." Accessed March 31, 2011. http:// www.evelyn.co.uk/hearing_essay.aspx.

Glover, John A., Royce R. Ronning, and Cecil R. Reynolds, eds. *Handbook of Creativity*. New York: Plenum.

Goldstein, Avram. 1980. "Thrills in Response to Music and Other Stimuli." *Physiological Psychology* 8 (1): 126–29.

Gopnik, Adam. 2010. "Van Gogh's Ear: The Christmas Eve That Changed Modern Art." *New Yorker*, January 4, 48–55.

Gordon, Edmund W., and Bridglall, Beatrice L. 2005. "Nurturing Talent in Gifted Students of Color." In *Conceptions of Giftedness*, 2nd ed., edited by Robert J. Sternberg and Janet E. Davidson, 120–46. New York: Cambridge University Press.

Gordon, Joanne, ed. 1997. *Stephen Sondheim: A Casebook*. New York: Garland Publishing.

Griffiths, Paul. 1998. "Of the Mind and Artists Who Lose It." *New York Times*, Arts section, July 28.

Grinder, Robert E. 1985. "The Gifted in Our Midst: By Their Divine Deeds, Neuroses, and Mental Test Scores We Have Known Them." In *The Gifted and Talented: Developmental Perspectives*, edited by Frances Horowitz and Marion O'Brien, 5–35. Washington, DC: American Psychological Association.

Grosskurth, Phyllis. 1997. *Byron: The Flawed Angel*. New York: Houghton Mifflin.

"Guiteaumania." 1882. *British Medical Journal*, June 24. 947–48.

Gural, Natasha. 2000. "Misbehaving Students Do Penance at Opera." AP report. *Journal News*, April 20, 45.

Gutin, Jo Ann C. 1996. "That Fine Madness: Manic Depression Is Latest Mental Illness Popularly Linked to Artistic Genius." *Discover*, October, 75–81.

Hamilton, E., and H. Cairns, eds. 1973. *The Collected Dialogues of Plato*. Princeton, NJ: Princeton University Press.

Hanna-Plady, Brenda, and Alicia MacKay. 2011. "The Relation between Instrumental Music Activity and Cognitive Aging." *Neuropsychology*, April 4. doi: 10.1037/a0021895.

Hanser, Suzanne. 1983. "Music Therapy: A Behavioral Perspective." *Behavior Therapist* 6 (1): 5–8.

Hargreaves, David J., and Adrian C. North. 1998. *The Social Psychology of Music*. New York: Oxford University Press.

Harris, Gardiner. 2008a. "Top Psychiatrist Didn't Report Drug Makers' Pay." *New York Times*, October 4. http://www.nytimes.com/2008/10/04/health/policy/04drug.html.

———. 2008b. "Use of Antipsychotics in Children Is Criticized." *New York Times*, November 19. http://www.nytimes.com/2008/11/19/health/policy/19fda.html.

———. 2009. "Drug Maker Told Studies Would Aid It, Papers Say." *New York Times*, March 20. http://www.nytimes.com/2009/03/20/us/20psych.html.

Harris, Gardiner, and Janet Roberts. 2006. "Proof Is Scant on Psychiatric Drug Mix for Young." *New York Times*, November 23. http://www.nytimes.com.

———. 2007a. "After Sanctions, Doctors Get Drug Company Pay." *New York Times*, June 3. http://www.nytimes.com/2007/06/03/health/03docs.html.

———. 2007b. "Doctors' Ties to Drug Makers Are Put on Close View." *New York Times*, March 21. http://www.nytimes.com.

Hart, Mickey, and Fredric Lieberman. 1991. *Planet Drum: A Celebration of Percussion and Rhythm*. New York: HarperCollins.

Hayden, Deborah. 2003. *Pox: Genius, Madness, and the Mysteries of Syphilis*. New York: Basic Books.

Hayes, John R. 1989. "Cognitive Processes in Creativity." In *Handbook of Creativity*, edited by John A. Glover, Royce R. Ronning, and Cecil R. Reynolds, 135–45. New York: Plenum.

Healy, Melissa. 2007. "Are We Too Quick to Medicate Children?" *LA Times*, November 5.

Helfgott, David. 1998. Bravo profile aired June 14.

———. 2010. "David Helgott Still Shines." Interview of David on Australian television by entertainment editor Fifi Box, August. http://au.tv.yahoo.com/sunrise/video/-/watch/21436480.

Helfgott, Margaret. 1998a. *Out of Tune: David Helfgott and the Myth of Shine*. New York: Warner Books.

———. 1998b. Personal communication, July 28.

Hennessey, Beth A. 2010. "The Creativity-Motivation Connection." In Kaufman and Sternberg 2010, 342–65.

Hennessey, Beth A., and Teresa M. Amabile 1998. "Reward, Intrinsic Motivation, and Creativity." *American Psychologist* 53 (June): 674–75.

Hentoff, Nat. 1991. *Jazz Is*. New York: Random House.

Hershman, D. Jablow, and Julian Lieb. 1988. *The Key to Genius: Manic-Depression and the Creative Life*. New York: Prometheus Books.

Hinshaw, Stephen P. 2007. *The Mark of Shame: Stigma of Mental Illness and an Agenda for Change*. New York: Oxford University Press.

Holden, Constance. 1987. "Creativity and the Troubled Mind." *Psychology Today*, April, 9–10.

Holyoak, Keith J., and Robert G. Morrison, eds. 2005. *Cambridge Handbook of Thinking and Reasoning*. New York: Cambridge University Press.

Horowitz, Frances Degan, and Marion O'Brien, eds. 1985. *The Gifted and Talented: Developmental Perspectives*. Washington, DC: The American Psychological Association.

Horwitz, Allan V. 2002. *Creating Mental Illness*. Chicago: University of Chicago Press.

Huff, Darrell. 1993. *How to Lie with Statistics*. New York: W. W. Norton.

Huneker, James Gibbons. 1900. *Chopin: The Man and His Music*. New York: Charles Scribner's Sons.

Hunter, Richard, and Ida Macalpine. 1982. *Three Hundred Years of Psychiatry 1535–1860: A History Presented in Selected English Texts*. Hartsdale, NY: Carlisle Publishing.

Hyman, Steven E. 2011. "Diagnosing the DSM: Diagnostic Classification Needs Fundamental Reform." The Dana Foundation, April 26.

Hyslop, Theophilius Bulkeley. 1925. *The Great Abnormals*. New York: George H. Doran Company.

International Society of Affective Disorders (ISAD) Institute of Psychiatry, De Crespigny Park, London Se5 8AF, England.

"Is Genius Insanity? Phrenological and Other Methods in an Interesting Problem." 1913. *New York Times*, April 20. http://www.nytimes.com.

Israels, Chuck. 2001. Personal communication, August 30.

James, Jamie. 1994. "Though This Were Madness, Was There Yet Method in 'T?" *New York Times*, August 7, 27–28.

James, William. (1901–1902) 2010. *The Varieties of Religious Experience: A Study in Human Nature: Being the Gifford Lectures on Natural Religion Delivered at Edinburgh in 1901–1902*. New York: Library of America Paperback Classics.

Jamison, Kay Redfield. 1988a. *Moods and Music*. Producer and speaker. Concert featuring the works of composers with manic-depressive illness. Performed by the National Symphony Orchestra at the John F. Kennedy Center for the Performing Arts. Washington, DC, November. (Also performed by the Los Angeles Philharmonic with pianist and coproducer Robert Winter, May 19, 1985.)

———. 1988b. *Moods and Music*. Sixty-minute video. Executive producer and writer. Public Broadcasting Service television special. National broadcast November 1989.

———. 1989. "Mood Disorders and Patterns of Creativity in British Writers and Artists." *Psychiatry* 52: 125–34.

———. 1993. *Touched with Fire: Manic-Depressive Illness and the Artistic Temperament*. New York: Free Press.

———. 1994. "The Inner World of Robert Schumann: Manic Depression and the Creative Process." (Moderator) Bard Music Festival, Bard College, Annandale-on-Hudson, NY, August 14.

———. 1995a. "Manic-Depressive Illness and Creativity." *Scientific American* 272 (February): 62–67.

———. 1995b. *An Unquiet Mind: A Memoir of Moods and Madness*. New York: Alfred A. Knopf.

———. 1998. Live from Lincoln Center interview (see also Masur and Chang). www.livefromlincolncenter.org/backstage/march3.jamison,html.

———. 2002. *Introduction to Unholy Ghost: Writers on Depression*. Edited by Nell Casey, 1–7. New York: Harper Perennial.

———. 2003. Invited address to the Writers' Guild (West) August. Accessed August 13, 2007.www.wga.org/health/jamison/touchedfull.

———. 2004a. *Exuberance: The Passion for Life*. New York: Alfred A. Knopf.

———. 2004b. "A Passion for Life?" Letter to the editor. *New York Times Book Review*, December 26, 5.

———. 2005. "The View from Here: Wild Unrest." *Poetry*, December, 225–27.

———. 2010. Liner notes to *Singing in the Dark*, Susan McKeown CD. New York: Hibernian Music. Onstage remarks at the CD launch, Symphony Space, New York, NY, October 30.

Janofsky, Michael. 1997. "Attention, Snuff Eaters: See a Shrink." *New York Times Week in Review*, November 16, 47.

Jenkins, Todd. 2008. "High Tide: Bud Shank Keeps Blowing His Distinctive West Coast Style." *DownBeat*, May, 52–53.

Johnson, Paul. 2000. *The Renaissance: A Short History*. New York: The Modern Library.

Jones, Mari Riess, and Susan Holleran. 1992. *Cognitive Bases of Musical Communication*. Washington, DC: American Psychological Association.

Joseph, Jay. 2004. "More Mythmaking in Psychiatric Genetic Research." *Ethical Human Psychology and Psychiatry* 6 (4): 231–32.

Jourdain, Robert. 2002. *Music, the Brain, and Ecstasy: How Music Captures Our Imagination*. New York: HarperCollins.

Juda, Adele. 1949. "The Relationship between Highest Mental Capacity and Psychic Abnormalities." *American Journal of Psychiatry* 106 (October): 296–307.

Juni, Samuel, Susan P. Nelson, and Robert Brannon. 1987. "Minor Tonality Music Preference and Oral Dependency." *Journal of Psychology* 121 (3): 229–36.

Juslin, Patrik N., and John A. Sloboda, eds. 2001. *Music and Emotion: Theory and Research*. New York: Oxford University Press.

Kagan, Jerome. 2008. "The Meaning of Psychological Abnormality." *Cerebrum*, November 10. http://www.dana.org/news/cerebrum/detail.aspx?id=13800.

Kaufman, James C., and Robert J. Sternberg, eds. 2010. *The Cambridge Handbook of Creativity*. New York: Cambridge University Press.

Kelley, Robin D. G. 2009. *Thelonious Monk: The Life and Times of an American Original*. New York: Free Press.

Kemp, Anthony E. 1996. *The Musical Temperament: Psychology and Personality of Musicians*. New York: Oxford University Press.

Kenny, Dianna T., Justine Cormack, and Rosemary Martin. 2009. "Suffering for One's Art: Performance Related Musculoskeletal Disorders in Tertiary Performing Arts Students in Music and Dance." In *Proceedings of the International Symposium on Performance Science*, edited by Aaron Williamon, Sharman Pretty, and Ralph Buck, 25–30. Utrecht, The Netherlands: European Association of Conservatoires (AEC).

Kerlinger, Fred N. 1973. *Foundations of Behavioral Research*. 2nd ed. New York: Holt, Rinehart and Winston.

Kershaw, Sarah. 2010. "Mental Health Experts Applaud Focus on Parity." *New York Times*, March 30, D5.

Kessel, Neil. 1989. "Genius and Mental Disorder: A History of Ideas Concerning Their Conjunction." In *Genius: The History of an Idea*, edited by Patricia Murray, 196–212. New York: Basil Blackwell.

Keynes, M. 1980. "Handel's Illnesses." *Lancet* 20 (27): 1354–55.

Kim, Nancy S., and Woo-kyoung Ahn. 2002. "Clinical Psychologists' Theory-Based Representations of Mental Disorders Predict Their Diagnostic Reasoning and Memory." *Journal of Experimental Psychology: General* 131 (4): 451–76.

Kivy, Peter. 2001. *The Possessor and the Possessed: Handel, Mozart, Beethoven, and the Idea of Musical Genius*. New Haven: Yale University Press.

Kounios, J., and M. Jung-Beeman. 2009. "Aha! The Cognitive Neuroscience of Insight." *Current Directions in Psychological Science* 18: 210–16.

Kowalczyk, Liz. 2009. "Senator Broadens Inquiry into Psychiatrist: Suggests MGH Doctor Was Biased in Research." *Boston Globe*, March 21.

Kposowa, A. J. 1999. "Suicide Mortality in the United States: Differentials by Industrial and Occupational Groups." *American Journal of Independent Medicine* 36 (6): 645–52.

Kramer, Peter D. 2005. "There's Nothing Deep about Depression: Why Do We Continue to Believe That Clinical Depression Brings with It Artistic Insight and Literary Greatness?" *New York Times Magazine*, April 17, 50–54.

Kretschmer, Ernst. 1925. *Physique and Character: An Investigation of the Nature of Constitution and of the Theory of Temperament*. Translated by W. J. H. Sprott. London: Kegan Paul, Trench & Trubner. Google Books.

———. 1931. *The Psychology of Men of Genius*. Translated, with an introduction, by R. B. Cattell. New York: Harcourt Brace and Company.

Krieger, Sarah. 1994. Personal communication, March 15.

Kris, Ernst, and Otto Kurz. 1979. *Legend, Myth, and Magic in the Image of the Artist: A Historical Experiment*. New Haven: Yale University Press.

Kutchins, Herb, and Stuart A. Kirk. 1997. *Making Us Crazy: DSM: The Psychiatric Bible and the Creation of Mental Disorders*. New York: Free Press.

Lacasse, Jeffrey R. 2005. "Consumer Advertising of Psychiatric Medications Biases the Public against Nonpharmacological Treatment." *Ethical Human Psychology and Psychiatry* 7 (3): 175–79.

Lahr, John. 1999. "Profile: The Demon-Lover (Ingmar Bergman)." *New Yorker*, May 31, 67–79.

Landers, Ann. 2000. "Gem of the Day." *Journal News*, September 22, 6E.

Lane, Christopher. 2007. *Shyness: How Normal Behavior Became a Sickness*. New Haven, CT: Yale University Press.

Lange-Eichbaum, Wilhelm. 1932. *The Problem of Genius*. New York: Macmillan.

Lebrecht, Norman. 1982. *Discord: Conflict and the Making of Music*. London: Andre Deutsch Limited.

Lees, Gene. 1987. *Singers and the Song*. New York: Oxford University Press.

———. 1998. Personal communication, August 4.

———. 2001. *You Can't Steal a Gift: Dizzy, Clark, Milt, and Nat*. New Haven: Yale University Press.

———. 2002. "Afterthoughts." *Jazzletter*, August, 21, 8.

———. 2003. Personal communication, April 4.

Lehmann-Haupt, Christopher. 2001. "Anthony Storr, 80, Psychiatrist and Writer" (obituary). *New York Times*, March 28, C21.

Leo, John. 1984. "The Ups and Downs of Creativity: Genius and Emotional Disturbance Are Linked in a New Study." *Time*, October 8, 76–77.

Lipton, Jack P. 1987. "Stereotypes Concerning Musicians within Symphony Orchestras." *Journal of Psychology* 121 (1): 85–93.

Lish, Jennifer D., Susan Dime-Meenan, Peter C. Whybrow, R. Arlen Price, and Robert M. A. Hirschfeld. 1994. "The National Depressive and Manic-Depressive Association (DMDA) Survey of Bipolar Members." *Journal of Affective Disorders* 31: 281–94.

Liszt, Franz. (1857) 1963. *Frederick Chopin*. Translated by Edward N. Waters. New York: Vienna House.

Loewenberg, Richard D. 1950. "Wilhelm Lange-Eichbaum and the Problem of Genius." *American Journal of Psychiatry*. 106 (June): 927–28. http://ajp.psychiatryonline.org/data/Journals/AJP/2403/927.pdf.

Lombroso, Cesare. 1895. *The Man of Genius*. Contemporary Science Series. Edited by Havelock Ellis. London: Walter Scott. Whitefish, MT: Kessinger's Publishing Rare Reprints.

Lubin, Bernard, Marvin Zuckerman, Linda M. Breytspraak, Neil C. Bull, Ashok K. Gumbhir, and Christine M. Rinck. 1988. "Affects, Demographic Variables, and Health." *Journal of Clinical Psychology* 44 (2): 131–41.

Ludwig, Arnold M. 1995. *The Price of Greatness: Resolving the Creativity and Madness Controversy*. New York: The Guilford Press.

Luhrmann, T. M. 2000. *Of Two Minds: The Growing Disorder in American Psychiatry*. New York: Alfred A. Knopf.

Macaulay, Lord, and Samuel Thurber, ed. (1825) 1891. *Macaulay's Essays on Milton and Addison*. Boston: Norwood Press. Google Books.

"Mad Genius: Study Suggests Link between Psychosis and Creativity." 2009. *Science Daily*, September 29. http://www.sciencedaily.com.

Maisel, Eric. 2008. *The Van Gogh Blues: The Creative Person's Path through Depression*. Novato, CA: New World Library.

Malcolm, Janet. 1981. *Psychoanalysis: The Impossible Profession*. New York: Alfred A. Knopf.

Mansury, Isabelle M., and Safa Mohanna. 2011. "Epigenetics and the Human Brain: Where Nurture Meets Nature." *Cerebrum*, May. http://dana.org/news/cerebrum/detail.aspx?id=32670.

Marchand, Leslie A. 1957. *Byron: A Biography*. Vol. 2. New York: Alfred A. Knopf.

Marshall, Michael. 2011. "Fall of Roman Empire Linked to Wild Shifts in Climate." *New Scientist*, January 13. Accessed March 30, 2011. http://www.newscientist.com/article/dn19968-fall-of-roman-empire.

Martindale, Colin. 1998. "Creativity and the Brain: Arnheim Award Address." *Psychology and the Arts*, Winter: 5–9. Washington, DC: American Psychological Association.

———. 2003. Personal communication, March 12.

Masur, Kurt, and Sarah Chang. 1998. Interview with Dr. Kay Redfield Jamison. www.livefromlincolncenter.org/backstage/march3.jamison,html.

May, Rollo. 1975. *The Courage to Create*. New York: W. W. Norton.

Mayne, Ethel Colburn. 1912. *Byron*. Vol. 1. New York: Charles Scribner's Sons. Google Books.

McDermott, Kathleen. 2001. "The Complexities of Self-Report." *Contemporary Psychology* 46 (3): 244–46.

Meltzer, H., Griffiths, C., Brock, A., Rooney, C., and R. Jenkins. 2008. "Patterns of Suicide by Occupation in England and Wales: 2001–2005." *British Journal of Psychiatry* 193 (1): 73–76.

Menuhin, Yehudi, and Curtis W. Davis. 1979. *The Music of Man*. New York: Simon & Schuster.

Merkin, Daphne. 2004a. "Ode to Joy." Review of *Exuberance: The Passion for Life* by Kay Redfield Jamison." *New York Times Book Review*, December 5, 56.

———. 2004b. Response to Kay Redfield Jamison's criticism of Merkin's Exuberance review. *New York Times Book Review*, December 26, 5.

Metheny, Mike. 2001. Personal communication, May 8.

Meyer, Leonard B. 1956. *Emotion and Meaning in Music*. Chicago: University of Chicago Press.

Miller, Paul R. 1995. "Diagnosis and Serendipity." The *American Journal of Psychiatry* 152 (10): 1530.

Mischel, Walter. 2009. "Editorial: Connecting Clinical Practice to Scientific Progress." *Psychological Science in the Public Interest* 9 (2): i.

Mitchell, Helen F., and Raymond A. R. MacDonald. 2009. "Linguistic Limitations of Describing Sound: Is Talking about Music like Dancing about Architecture?" In *Proceedings of the International Symposium on Performance Science*, edited by Aaron Williamon, Sharman Pretty, and Ralph Buck, 45–50. Utrecht, The Netherlands: European Association of Conservatoires (AEC).

Monroe, Russell R. 1992. *Creative Brainstorms: The Relationship between Madness and Genius.* New York: Irvington Publishers.

Morella, Joseph, and George Mazzei. 1996. *Genius & Lust: The Creative and Sexual Lives of Cole Porter and Noel Coward.* London: Robson Books.

Murray, Penelope, ed. 1989. *Genius: The History of an Idea.* New York: Basil Blackwell.

Mustard, C. A., A. Bielecky, J. Etches, R. Wilkins, M. Tiepkema, B. C. Amick, P. M. Smith, W. H. Gnam, and K. J. Aronson. 2010. "Suicide Mortality by Occupation in Canada, 1991–2001." *Canadian Journal of Psychiatry* 55 (6): 369–76.

Nakamura, Jeanne, and Mihaly Csikszentmihalyi. 2001. "Catalytic Creativity: The Case of Linus Pauling." *American Psychologist* 56 (4): 337–41.

NAMI National Depression Survey. 2005.

National Endowment for the Arts (NEA). 2003. "Changing the Beat: A Study of the Worklife of Jazz Musicians." NEA Research Division Report #43, vol 1. Executive Summary. Washington, DC.

Naughton, Jim. 2001. "Media Watch—No Shades of Gray: Examining the Media Bias toward the Sensational." *Psychotherapy Networker,* September/October: 19–20.

Nesse, Randolph. 1998. Mood Disorders: An Overview Part II. *Harvard Mental Health Letter* 14 (7): 1–7.

Nettle, Daniel. 2001. *Strong Imagination: Madness, Creativity, and Human Nature.* London: Oxford University Press.

Neugeboren, Jay. 1999. *Transforming Madness: New Lives for People Living with Mental Illness.* New York: William Morrow.

Neumeister, Kristie, L. Spiers, and Bonnie Cramond. 2004. "Obituary: E. Paul Torrance (1915–2003)." *American Psychologist* 59 (3): 179.

Nisbet, John F. (1891) 2010. *The Insanity of Genius and the General Inequality of Human Faculty:Physiologically Considered.* London: Ward & Downey. Historical reproduction, Breinigsville, PA: Bibliolife.

Northwood, Heidi. 2010. Personal communication, July 28–29.

———. n. d. "The Melancholic Mean: The Aristotelian Problema XXX.1.

Paideia: Ancient Philosophy." http://www.bu.edu/wcp/Papers/Anci/ AnciNort.htm.

Oliver, Joan M., and M. E. Simmons. 1985. "Affective Disorders and Depression as Measured by the Diagnostic Interview Schedule and the Beck Depression Inventory in an Unselected Adult Population." *Journal of Clinical Psychology* 41 (4): 469–77.

Osborne, Mary Pope. 2007. *Monday with a Mad Genius.* Magic Tree House series, no. 38. A Stepping Stone Book. New York: Random House Children's Books.

Osborne, Mary Pope, and Natalie Pope Boyce. 2009. *Leonardo da Vinci: A Nonfiction Companion to Monday with a Mad Genius.* New York: Random House Children's Books.

Ostwald, Peter E. 1985. *Schumann: The Inner Voices of a Musical Genius.* Boston: Northeastern University Press.

Padel, Ruth. 1995. *Whom Gods Destroy: Elements of Greek and Tragic Madness.* Princeton, NJ: Princeton University Press.

Perkins, David, ed. 1967. *English Romantic Writers.* New York: Harcourt, Brace & World.

Pfeiffer, Ernst, ed. 1972. *Sigmund Freud and Lou Andreas-Salomé Letters.* New York: Harcourt Brace Jovanovich.

Pickover, Clifford A. 1998a. "The Genius and the Nut: Embracing Disordered Brilliance." *Utne Reader*, July/August, 79.

———. 1998b. *Strange Brains and Genius.* New York: Plenum.

Plato. 2002. *Phaedrus.* Translated by Robin Waterfield. New York: Oxford University Press.

Plucker, Jonathan A., Ronald A. Beghetto, and Gayle T. Dow. 2004. "Why Isn't Creativity More Important to Educational Psychologists?" *Educational Psychology* 39: 83–96.

Plucker, Jonathan A., and Jacob J. Levy. 2001. "The Downside of Being Talented." *American Psychologist* 56 (1): 75–76.

Plucker, Jonathan A., and Matthew C. Makel. 2010. "Assessment of Creativity." In Kaufman and Sternberg 2010, 48–73.

Popper, Karl. 1963. *Conjectures and Refutations: The Growth of Scientific Knowledge.* New York: Routledge.

Porter, Roy. 1989. *A Social History of Madness: The World through the Eyes of the Insane.* New York: E. P. Dutton.

———. 2002. *Madness: A Brief History.* New York: Oxford University Press.

Post, Felix. 1994. "Creativity and Psychopathology: A Study of 291 World-Famous Men." *British Journal of Psychiatry* 165: 22–34.

President's New Freedom Commission on Mental Health. 2003. "March 2003

Meeting Minutes: Early Mental Health Screening and Treatment in Multiple Settings." Accessed August 17, 2011. http://govinfo.library.unt.edu/mentalhealthcommission/minutes/april03.htm.

Radden, Jennifer, ed. 2000. *The Nature of Melancholy from Aristotle to Kristeva.* New York: Oxford University Press.

Ratey, John J., and Catherine Johnson. 1997. *Shadow Syndromes: The Mild Forms of Major Mental Disorders That Sabotage Us.* New York: Bantam Books.

Ratliff, Ben. 2000. "Fixing, for Now, the Image of Jazz." *New York Times*, January 7, 1, 32.

Rehak, Melanie. 1999. "The Most Exquisite Clay Feet." *New York Times*, February 28, 26.

Rhead, John. 2004. "Some Dynamics of Psychological Reactions to Encountering Madness in Others." *Contemporary Psychology* 49 (2): 219–21.

Richards, Ruth. 1992. "Mood Swings and Everyday Creativity." *Harvard Mental Health Letter* 8 (10): 4–6.

———, ed. 2009. *Everyday Creativity and New Views of Human Nature: Psychological, Social and Spiritual Perspectives.* Washington, DC: American Psychological Association.

Roazen, Paul. 1993. *Meeting Freud's Family.* Amherst: University of Massachusetts Press.

Roberts, Michelle. 2010. "Creative Minds 'Mimic Schizophrenia.'" BBC News online, May 29. http://news.bbc.co.uk/2/hi/health/10154775.stm.

Rosen, Alan, and Garry Walter. 2000. "Way Out of Tune: Lessons from Shine and Its Exposé." *Australian and New Zealand Journal of Psychiatry* 34: 237–44.

Rosen, George. 1969. *Madness in Society: Chapters in the Historical Sociology of Mental Illness.* Chicago: University of Chicago Press.

Rosenhan, David. 1973. "On Being Sane in Insane Places." *Science*, n.s., 179 (4070): 250–58.

Rothenberg, Albert. 1990. *Creativity and Madness: New Findings and Old Stereotypes.* John Hopkins University Press.

Rouget, Gilbert. 1985. *Music and Trance: A Theory of the Relations between Music and Possession.* Chicago: University of Chicago Press.

Ruitenbeek, Hendrick M., ed. 1978. *Freud as We Knew Him.* Detroit: Wayne State University Press.

Runyan, William McKinley. 1981. "Why Did Van Gogh Cut Off His Ear? The Problem of Alternative Explanations in Psychobiography." *Journal of Personality and Social Psychology* 40 (6): 1070–77.

———. 1982. "In Defense of the Case Study Method." *American Journal of Orthopsychiatry* 52 (3): 440–46.

Sachs, Gary. 2001. Personal communication, July 24.

Sachs, Harvey. 2010. *The Ninth: Beethoven and the World in 1824*. New York: Random House.

Sacks, Oliver. 2007a. Lecture on "Music and the Mind" at the 92nd Street Y, New York City, April 24.

Sadie, Stanley, ed. 1988. *The Norton/Grove Concise Encyclopedia of Music*. New York: W. W. Norton.

Saeman, Henry. 2002. "New Mexico First to Pass Prescription Privileges." *National Psychologist* 11 (March/April): 2.

Sandblom, Philip. 1997. *Creativity and Disease: How Illness Affects Literature, Art, and Music*. 10th ed. New York: Marion Boyars Publishers.

Sandke, Randy. 2010. Personal communication, September 29.

Sarbin, Theodore R., and James C. Mancuso. 1980. *Schizophrenia: Medical Diagnosis or Moral Verdict?* Elmsford, NY: Pergamon Press.

Sarton, May. (1965) 1993. *Mrs. Stevens Hears the Mermaids Singing*. New York: W. W. Norton.

Sawyer, R. Keith. 2006. *Explaining Creativity: The Science of Human Innovation*. New York: Oxford University Press.

Schlesinger, Judith. 1997a. "Craziness Is Not the Price Paid for Genius." *Baltimore Sun*, April 6, 1F, 4F.

———. 1997b. "Psychology, Evil, and *Sweeney Todd*, or, 'Don't I Know You, Mister?'" In *Stephen Sondheim: A Casebook*, edited by Joanne Gordon, 125–41. New York: Garland Publishing.

———. 1998a. "Music and Madness." *Jazzletter* 17 (5): 1.

———. 1998b. "Review of 'Side Man.'" *Jazzletter* 17 (12): 2.

———. 1999a. "Chasing the Moment: Monty Alexander." Jazz Institute of Chicago. December 4. http://www.jazzinchicago.org/educates/journal/interviews/chasing-moment-monty-alexander.

———. 1999b. "The Epidemic of Ritalin: A Cure for Brattiness?" *Baltimore Sun*, January 17, 36. Accessed May 23, 2011. http://articles.baltimoresun.com.

———. 2000. "Critical Conditions." *Shrinktunes* column, Allaboutjazz.com. http://www.allaboutjazz.com/php/review_print.php?id=861.

———. 2001a. "An Old Story: Psychiatry Squashing Creativity, Freedom, Author Asserts." *National Psychologist*, July/August: 14–15.

———. 2001b. "Oppression by Psychiatry Is Not Unique to Tyrannies." *Baltimore Sun*, May 13, 11.

———. 2002a. "Issues in Creativity and Madness: Part One: Ancient Questions, Modern Answers." *Ethical Human Sciences and Services: An International Journal of Critical Inquiry*. 4 (1): 73–76.

———. 2002b. "Issues in Creativity and Madness: Part Two: Eternal Flames." *Ethical Human Sciences and Services: An International Journal of Critical Inquiry* 4 (2): 139–42.

———. 2002c. "The *Jazz Times* Halloween Scare." *Shrinktunes* column, All aboutjazz.com. December 3. http://www.allaboutjazz.com.

———. 2002d. "Mad in America: Beware Chemistry." *Baltimore Sun.* February 10.

———. 2003. "Issues in Creativity and Madness: Part Three: Who Cares?" *Ethical Human Sciences and Services: An International Journal of Critical Inquiry* 5 (2): 149–52.

———. 2004a. "Creativity and Mental Health." *British Journal of Psychiatry* 184 (February): 184–85.

———. 2004b. "Heroic, Not Disordered: Creativity and Mental Illness Revisited." *British Journal of Psychiatry* 184 (April): 363–64.

———. 2009. "Creative Mythconceptions: A Closer Look at the Evidence for the Mad Genius Hypothesis." *Psychology of Aesthetics, Creativity, and the Arts* 3 (2): 62–72.

———. 2010. "Mad and Genius Are Separate States of Mind." *National Psychologist* 19 (3): 13.

———. Forthcoming. "Building Connections on Sand: The Cautionary Chapter." In *Creativity and Mental Illness*, edited by James C. Kaufman. Cambridge: Cambridge University Press.

Schneider, Daniel E. 1950. *The Psychoanalyst and the Artist.* New York: Farrar, Straus and Company.

Schulze, Thomas G. 2010. "Genetic Research into Bipolar Disorder: The Need for a Research Framework That Integrates Sophisticated Molecular Biology and Clinically Informed Phenotype Characterization." *Psychiatric Clinics of North America* 33 (1): 67–82.

Schwarz, Norbert. 1999. "Self-Reports: How the Questions Shape the Answers." *American Psychologist* 54 (2): 93–105.

Seashore, Carl E. 1938. *Psychology of Music.* New York: Dover Publications.

———. 1951. *Why We Love Music.* Philadelphia, PA: Oliver Ditson Company.

Seligman, Martin. 2011a. *Flourish: A Visionary New Understanding of Happiness and Well-Being.* New York: Free Press.

———. 2011b. Personal communication, January 24.

Seligman, Martin, and Christopher Peterson. 2004. *Character Strengths and Virtues: A Handbook and Classification.* New York: Oxford University Press.

Seneca, Lucius Annaeus. n.d. "On Tranquillity of Mind." In *Moral Essays*, sec. 17.10, as quoted in Bartlett 1992, 103.

Shaffer, Peter. 2000. "Mozart, Truth, and the Demands of Drama." *New York Times*, February 20, 5.

Shakespeare, William. (1594–1595) 1992. *A Midsummer Night's Dream*. New York: Dover Publications.

———. 1974. *The Merchant of Venice*. In *The Complete Works of William Shakespeare*, vol. 1, edited by W. G. Clark and W. Aldis Wright, 331–55. New York: Doubleday.

Shapero, Harold. 1985. "The Musical Mind." In *The Creative Process: A Symposium*, edited by Brewster Ghiselin, 41–45. Berkeley, CA: University of California Press.

Shaw, George Bernard. (1931) 1955. *Shaw on Music*. Edited by Eric Bentley. New York: Applause Books.

Shekerjian, Denise. 1990. *Uncommon Genius: How Great Ideas Are Born*. New York: Penguin Books.

Sidran, Ben. 1995. *Talking Jazz: An Oral History*. New York: Da Capo Press.

Silvia, Paul J., and James C. Kaufman. 2010. "Creativity and Mental Illness." In Kaufman and Sternberg 2010, 381–94.

Simonton, Dean Keith. 1986. "Presidential Personality: Biographical Use of the Gough Adjective Check List." *Journal of Personality and Social Psychology* 51 (1): 149–60.

———. 1990. *Psychology, Science, and History: An Introduction to Historiometry*. New Haven, Connecticut: Yale University Press.

———. 1994. *Greatness: Who Makes History and Why*. New York: The Guilford Press.

———. 2004. "Creativity as a Constrained Stochastic Process." In *Creativity: From Potential to Realization*, edited by Robert J. Sternberg et al., 83–101. Washington, DC: American Psychological Association.

Skultans, Vieda. 1979. *English Madness: Ideas on Insanity 1580–1890*. London: Routledge & Kegan Paul.

Sleek, Scott. 1996. "Ensuring Accuracy in Clinical Decisions: Psychologists Explore Ways to Make Their Diagnoses and Assessments as Accurate as Possible." *APA Monitor* (April): 30.

Sloboda, John A. 1985. *The Musical Mind: The Cognitive Psychology of Music*. London: Oxford University Press.

———. 1992. "Empirical Studies of Emotional Response to Music." In Jones and Holleran 1992, 33–46.

Smith, Daniel B. 2007. *Muses, Madmen, and Prophets: Rethinking the History, Science, and Meaning of Auditory Hallucination*. New York: The Penguin Press.

Smith, Jonathan. 2004. "Playing Jazz: An Experience of Flow." *Journal of Critical Psychology, Counselling and Psychotherapy* 4 (1): 44–53.

Solis, Gabriel. 2004. Personal communication, April 4.

Sondheim, Stephen. 1998. Personal communication, March 9.

Sonneck, O. G., ed. 1926. *Beethoven: Impressions by His Contemporaries.* New York: Dover Publications.

Spitzer, Robert. 2011. "Psychological Warfare: The DSM-5 Debate." Health Care Professionals Live, February. http://www.hcplive.com/publications/mdng-Neurology/2011.

Sternberg, Robert J., and Janet E. Davidson, eds. 2005. *Conceptions of Giftedness.* 2nd ed. New York: Cambridge University Press.

Sternberg, Robert J., James C. Kaufman, and Jean E. Pretz. 2002. *The Creativity Conundrum: A Propulsion Model of Kinds of Creative Contributions.* New York: Psychology Press.

Sternberg, Robert J., and Todd I. Lubart. 1995. *Defying the Crowd: Cultivating Creativity in a Culture of Conformity.* New York: The Free Press.

———. 1996."Investing in Creativity." *American Psychologist* 51 (7): 677–88.

Sternberg, Robert J., Todd I. Lubart, James C. Kaufman, and Jean E. Pretz. 2005. "Creativity." In *The Cambridge Handbook of Thinking and Reasoning,* edited by Keith J. Holyoak and Robert G. Morrisonn, 351–69. New York: Cambridge University Press.

Stolorow, Robert D., and George E. Atwood. 1979. *Faces in a Cloud: Subjectivity in Personality Theory.* New York: Jason Aronson.

Storr, Anthony. 1992. *Music and the Mind.* New York: Ballantine Books.

———. 1993. *The Dynamics of Creation.* New York: Ballantine Books.

Styron, William. 1990. *Darkness Visible: A Memoir of Madness.* New York: Random House.

Sudhalter, Richard M. 1996. "Faery Tales and Hero Worship." *Jazzletter* 15 (8): 1–2.

———. 1999. Composing the words that might capture jazz. *New York Times,* August 29, sec. 2, 1, and 24.

Sundararajan, Louise, and Averill, James R. 2006. "Creativity in the Everyday Culture, Self, and Emotions." In *Everyday Creativity and New Views of Human Nature: Psychological, Social, and Spiritual Perspectives,* edited by Ruth Richards, 195–220. Washington, DC: American Psychological Association.

Szasz, Thomas. 1987. *Insanity: The Idea and Its Consequences.* 1st ed. New York: John Wiley & Sons.

———. 2006. *My Madness Saved Me: The Madness and Marriage of Virginia Woolf.* New Brunswick, NJ: Transaction Publishers.

Tame, David. 1984. *The Secret Power of Music: The Transformation of Self and Society through Musical Energy*. Northamptonshire, England: Turnstone Press.

Taruskin, Richard. 2001. "Music's Dangers and the Case for Control." *New York Times*, December 9, sec. 2, 1, 34.

Taylor, Arthur. 1977. *Notes and Tones: Musician-to-Musician Interviews*. New York: Coward, McCann & Geoghegan.

Taylor, Kate. 2007. "Letters Give New View of Artist." *New York Sun*, August 21. http://www.nysun.com/article/60969.

Tharp, Twyla. 2003. *The Creative Habit: Learn it and Use It for Life*. New York: Simon & Schuster.

"This Is Your Brain on Jazz: Researchers Use MRI to Study Spontaneity, Creativity." 2008. Johns Hopkins Medicine news release, February 26.

Thomas, John. 2004. "Firewall Needed between Marketing and Science." *National Psychologist* 13 (5): 1, 5.

Thomas, Kadesha, and Robert Mitchum. 2010. "The Brain's Electrical Storm." *Medicine on the Midway*, Fall: 9–12. Chicago: University of Chicago Biological Services Division.

Torrance, E. Paul. 1983. Personal communication, November 10.

Van de Ven, Niels, Marcel Zeelenberg, and Rik Pieters. 2010. "Warding off the Evil Eye: When the Fear of Being Envied Increases Prosocial Behavior." *Psychological Science* 21 (11): 1671–77.

Vasquez, Gustavo, and Leonardo Tondo. 2007. "The Bipolar Spectrum: How Far Are We Going?" Meeting report, International Society for Affective Disorders (ISAD) Regional Meeting 2005. *Journal of Affective Disorders* 98: 173–75.

"Vincent van Gogh Mad Genius Gene Discovered by Scientists." 2009. *U.K. Mirror*, September 30. http://www.mirror.co.uk/news/uk-news/vincent-van-gogh-mad-genius-421766.

Von Karolyi, Catya, and Ellen Winner. 2005. "Extreme Giftedness." In *Conceptions of Giftedness*, 2nd ed., edited by Robert J. Sternberg and Janet Davidson, 377–94. New York: Cambridge University Press.

Wade, Nicholas. 2010. "A Decade Later, Genetic Map Yields Few New Cures." *New York Times*, June 12. http://www.nytimes.com.

Waldman, Amy. 2001. "More No-Nos Than You Can Shake a Stick At. (Hey, No Stick-Shaking.)" *New York Times Week in Review*, December 2. 7.

Wallace, Doris B. 1989. "Studying the Individual: The Case Study Method and Other Genres." In Wallace and Gruber 1989, 25–43.

Wallace, Doris B., and Howard E. Gruber. 1989. *Creative People at Work: Twelve Cognitive Case Studies*. New York: Oxford University Press.

Washburne, Christopher. 2004. "Does Kenny G Play Bad Jazz?" In *Bad Music:*

The Music We Love to Hate, edited by Christopher Washburne and Maiken Derno, 123–47. New York: Routledge.

Washburne, Christopher, and Maiken Derno, eds. 2004. *Bad Music: The Music We Love to Hate*. New York: Routledge.

Washington, Peter. 1995. *Madame Blavatsky's Baboon: A History of the Mystics, Mediums, and Misfits Who Brought Spiritualism to America*. New York: Schocken Books.

Watters, Ethan. 2010a. "The Americanization of Mental Illness." *New York Times*, January 10. http://www.nytimes.com/2010/01/10/magazine/10psyche-t.html.

———. 2010b. *Crazy Like Us: The Globalization of the American Psyche*. New York: Free Press.

Webb, James T., Edward R. Amend, Nadia E. Webb, Jean Goerss, Paul Beljan, and F. Richard Olenchak. 2004. *Misdiagnosis and Dual Diagnoses of Gifted Children and Adults: ADHD, Bipolar, OCD, Asperger's, Depression, and Other Disorders*. Scottsdale, Arizona: Great Potential Press.

Weisberg, Robert W. 1993. *Creativity: Beyond the Myth of Genius*. New York: W. H. Freeman & Company.

———. 2006. *Creativity: Understanding Innovation in Problem Solving, Science, Invention, and the Arts*. New York: John Wiley & Sons.

Wells, Peter S. 2009. *Barbarians to Angels: The Dark Ages Reconsidered*. New York: W. W. Norton.

Weston, Tim. 2002. Personal communication, April 11.

Westrup, Sir Jack, and F. Ll. Harrison. 1985. *Collins Encyclopedia of Music*. Revised by Conrad Wilson. London: William Collins & Sons.

"What Killed Rebecca Riley?" 2007. *60 Minutes* DVD. CBS Broadcasting.

Whitaker, Robert. 2002. *Mad in America: Bad Science, Bad Medicine, and the Enduring Mistreatment of the Mentally Ill*. Cambridge, MA: Perseus Publishing.

———. 2005. "Anatomy of an Epidemic: Psychiatric Drugs and the Astonishing Rise of Mental Illness in America." *Ethical Human Psychology and Psychiatry* (7) 1: 23–35.

White, Thomas W. 2004. "Correctional Psychology's Perfect Storm." *National Psychologist*, January/February: 11.

Williamon, Aaron, Sharman Pretty, and Ralph Buck, eds. 2009. "Proceedings of the International Symposium on Performance Science." Utrecht, The Netherlands: European Association of Conservatoires (AEC).

Williams, Kipling D., and Steve A. Nida. 2011. "Ostracism: Consequences and Coping." *Current Directions in Psychological Science* 20 (2): 71–75.

Wills, Geoffrey I. 2003. "Forty Lives in the Bebop Business: Mental Health in a Group of Eminent Jazz Musicians." *British Journal of Psychiatry* 183: 255–59.

———. 2004. "Wills's Reply [to Schlesinger]." *British Journal of Psychiatry* 184: 184–85.

Wills, Geoffrey I., and Cary L. Cooper. 1988. *Pressure Sensitive: Popular Musicians under Stress.* London, England: Sage Publications.

Winner, Ellen. 2004. "Musical Giftedness." In *Bulletin of Psychology and the Arts Special Issue: Psychology of Music.* American Psychological Association Division 10 4 (1): 2–5.

Wittkower, Rudolf, and Margot Wittkower. 1963. *Born under Saturn: The Character and Conduct of Artists.* New York: W. W. Norton.

Woods, Frederick Adams. 1911. *Historiometry as an Exact Science.* Pamphlet reprinted from *Science* 33 (850): 568–74.

"Worksheet: Is Your Child Bipolar?" 2002. *Time,* August 19. Accessed at *Time* online archive on March 3, 2011. http://www.time.com/time/covers/1101020819/worksheet.

Worthen, John. 2007. *Robert Schumann: Life and Death of a Musician.* New Haven: Yale University Press.

Wright, Wayne. 2004. Personal communication, December 6.

Yaffe, David. 1998. "The Latest of the Jazz Weirdos." *New York Times,* October 35, 41.

Zaslow, Jeffrey. 1996. "k. d. lang: Different Is OK." *USA Weekend,* February 16–18, 18.

Zhong, C. B., A. Dijksterhuis, and A. D. Galinsky. 2008. "The Merits of Unconscious Thought in Creativity." *Psychological Science* 19 (9): 912–18.

Index

About the Author

Judith Schlesinger has been a writer, singer, and classical pianist since childhood; more recent creative pursuits have included PhD psychologist and psychotherapist (twenty-six years and counting), college professor (seventeen years), book, culture, and jazz critic (two decades, fast approaching three), and CD producer and leader of the JS Fourtet (newest hats).

A member of the Association for Psychological Science, the Author's Guild, and the National Association of Science Writers, Judith's first book was a film biography of Humphrey Bogart (Metro, 1997); she was also invited to write the psychology chapter for *Stephen Sondheim: A Casebook* (Garland, 2000). Her numerous book reviews and essays on education, psychology, and society are archived at the *Baltimore Sun*.

Judith's work has appeared in the *American Psychologist*, the *National Psychologist*, the *Counseling Psychologist*, the *British Journal of Psychiatry*, *Ethical Human Psychology and Psychiatry*, the *Psychology of Aesthetics, Creativity and the Arts*, and the *Journal of Polymorphous Perversity*. She is one of the few psychologists to question the accepted link between creativity and madness.

Always passionate about music, Judith has also written for the *All Music Guide*, the Jazz Institute of Chicago, the *Jazzletter*, Jazz.com, and the *Encyclopedia of American Studies*. She is a senior reviewer and columnist for the world's premiere jazz website, All About Jazz, where her Shrinktunes column explores the overlap between jazz and psychology.

Judith lives in the Hudson Valley with her rescue dog, Diggit.

CPSIA information can be obtained at www.ICGtesting.com
Printed in the USA
LVOW06s0545271215

467669LV00091B/2487/P